Study Skills Strategies

Get the most from every minute of learning

Fourth Edition

Uelaine A. Lengefeld

A Crisp Fifty-Minute™ Series Book

AXZO PRESS

Study Skills Strategies

Get the most from every minute of learning

Fourth Edition

Uelaine A. Lengefeld

CREDITS:

President, Axzo Press:	**Jon Winder**
Vice President, Product Development:	**Charles G. Blum**
Vice President, Operations:	**Josh Pincus**
Director, Publishing Systems Development:	**Dan Quackenbush**
Developmental Editor:	**Jim O'Shea**
Copy Editor:	**Ken Maher**

Trademarks

Crisp Fifty-Minute Series is a trademark of Axzo Press.

Some of the product names and company names used in this book have been used for identification purposes only and may be trademarks or registered trademarks of their respective manufacturers and sellers.

Disclaimer

We reserve the right to revise this publication and make changes from time to time in its content without notice.

ISBN 10: 1-4260-1832-0
ISBN 13: 978-1-4260-1832-9

Printed in the United States of America

1 2 3 4 5 6 7 8 9 10 12 11 10 09

Table of Contents

About the Author

Uelaine Lengefeld spent more than 40 years as a high school, community college, and university instructor and administrator. She was chairperson of the English Department at Claremont High School, honored as the San Gabriel Teacher of the Year, and nominated for State Teacher of the Year in California. In addition, she taught study skills and coordinated the Educational Opportunity Program (EOP) Instructional Support Center at Cal Poly State University in Pomona, California.

Later, she was director of the Learning Center and supervisor of the Disabled Students Program at Citrus Community College in Glendora, California. She also taught English and ESL (English as Second Language) at Citrus. She is now retired from teaching.

Previous editions of *Study Skills Strategies* have been translated into seventeen other languages.

Preface

Fear of the unknown is both normal and healthy. It can be a powerful motivator. On the other hand, too much fear can cause procrastination and sometimes paralysis. If you learn proven study skills strategies, much of the fear about college, or any new learning experience, will fade.

This book will help you design a study improvement plan based on your skills, needs, and individual situation. Whether you study full time or part time, whatever your age, background, or culture, you will find suggestions for tailoring your study plan to give you the best advantage for successful learning. Your anxiety will diminish and your confidence will grow once you are familiar with the study skills in this book.

You'll find that you're able to focus more clearly on important points and organize your note-taking, reading, and review work for more effective learning. This new edition includes tips for using technology to enhance these skills and others for online learning. You'll also find suggestions for getting assistance with any special needs you have.

Achieving all of this will take effort on your part, but if you're serious about your studies, it will be well worth the time you invest.

Your Learning Strategies Coach,

Uelaine A Lengefeld

Uelaine A. Lengefeld

Acknowledgments

Special thanks go to the late Elwood Chapman for his ideas and for his special mentoring throughout the creation of the first edition. Michael Crisp's talented editorial pen was essential, and I'm grateful for his original assistance.

I also want to acknowledge Professors Walter Lilian Metlitzky, Martha Maxwell, Frank Robinson, Frank Christ, Shuling Cummins, and Colin Rose for research contributions in the field of learning and reading skills.

Also, special appreciation in the Third Edition goes to Debbie Woodbury for her guidance and to Marguerite Langlois for her insight on new and emerging study issues for today's learners.

Special thanks to the expertise, guidance, and support of Charlie Blum, VP of Product Development, Adam Wilcox, and Jim O'Shea.

I want to thank Linda Giammanco especially for her computer skills and patient support during the entire publishing process of the Fourth Edition. Without her help, this edition would not have come to fruition.

Dedication

With love for Katherine Lorraine Leung who has lovingly supported me throughout the development of this edition.

Also, this book is dedicated to Gwyneth Amber Leung and Logan Christopher Leung. Gwyneth, age 8, has suggested "to improve your sentences, they should make sense and be understandable." She loves to write and wants to be like her grandmother and publish a book.

Learning Objectives

Complete this book, and you'll know how to:

1) Assess study skills and plan for improvement

2) Practice time-management techniques for successful studying

3) Take clear, meaningful classroom notes and study effectively from them

4) Use the five-step method to develop powerful reading skills

5) Practice memory techniques to enhance ability to learn

6) Improve test performance

7) Develop specific study skills for mathematics and related subjects

8) Review your study skills and implement an action plan to improve them

Workplace and Management Competencies mapping

For over 30 years, business and industry has utilized competency models to select employees. The trend to use competency-based approaches in education and training, assessment, and development of workers has experienced a more recent emergence within the Employment and Training Administration (ETA), a division of the United States Department of Labor.

The ETA's General Competency Model Framework spans a wide array of competencies from the more basic competencies, such as reading and writing, to more advanced occupation-specific competencies. The Crisp Series finds its home in what the ETA refers to as the Workplace Competencies and the Management Competencies.

Study Skills Strategies covers information vital to mastering the following competencies:

Workplace Competencies:

▶ Planning & Organizing

▶ Scheduling & Coordinating

For a comprehensive mapping of Crisp Series titles to the Workplace and Management competencies, visit www.CrispSeries.com.

About the Crisp 50-Minute Series

The Crisp 50-Minute Series was designed to cover critical business and professional development topics in the shortest possible time. Our easy-to-read, easy-to-understand format can be used for self-study or for classroom training. With a wealth of hands-on exercises, the 50-Minute books keep you engaged and help you retain critical skills.

What You Need to Know

We designed the Crisp 50-Minute Series to be as self-explanatory as possible. But there are a few things you should know before you begin the book.

Exercises

Exercises look like this:

EXERCISE TITLE

Questions and other information would be here.

Keep a pencil handy. Any time you see an exercise, you should try to complete it. If the exercise has specific answers, an answer key is provided in the appendix. (Some exercises ask you to think about your own opinions or situation; these types of exercises don't have answer keys.)

Forms

A heading like this means that the rest of the page is a form:

FORMHEAD

Forms are meant to be reusable. You might want to make a photocopy of a form before you fill it out, so that you can use it again later.

A Note to Instructors

We've tried to make the Crisp 50-Minute Series books as useful as possible as classroom training manuals. Here are some of the features we provide for instructors:

▶ PowerPoint presentations

▶ Answer keys

▶ Assessments

▶ Customization

PowerPoint Presentations

You can download a PowerPoint presentation for this book from our Web site at www.CrispSeries.com.

Answer keys

If an exercise has specific answers, an answer key will be provided in the appendix. (Some exercises ask you to think about your own opinions or situation; these types of exercises will not have answer keys.)

Assessments

For each 50-Minute Series book, we have developed a 35- to 50-item assessment. The assessment for this book is available at www.CrispSeries.com. *Assessments should not be used in any employee-selection process.*

Customization

Crisp books can be quickly and easily customized to meet your needs—from adding your logo to developing proprietary content. Crisp books are available in print and electronic form. For more information on customization, see www.CrispSeries.com.

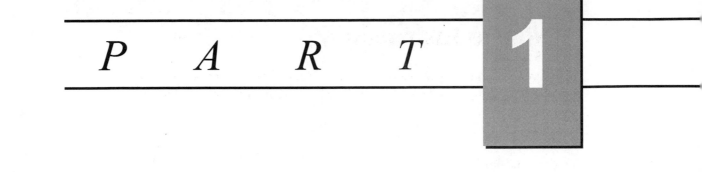

P A R T 1

Getting Started

In this part:

▶ Discover Your Attitude toward Learning

▶ Today's Diverse Classrooms

▶ Computers as Learning Tools

▶ Your Focus Points

Discover Your Attitude Toward Learning

To learn and apply quality study skills, it's essential to have a positive attitude. In fact, your attitude and motivation will make all the difference. To measure your attitude toward studying, complete this exercise.

YOUR ATTITUDE TOWARD LEARNING

Read each statement. Check Yes (Y) if it describes your attitude or study habit. If it doesn't, check No (N). Be honest.

Attitudes	Y	N
1. I'm satisfied with my test scores on most examinations.	❏	❏
2. If I do poorly on a test, I increase my efforts and get help from a teacher, a tutor, or a study partner.	❏	❏
3. When required, I can concentrate on studies. I'm not easily distracted.	❏	❏
4. The challenge of taking study notes on difficult textbook reading doesn't throw me.	❏	❏
5. Although busy, I'm able to find priority time to study. Procrastination and cramming aren't problems for me.	❏	❏
6. I attend class regularly and carefully prepare for most class sessions.	❏	❏
7. I have a clear reason for going to school, and I know that good study skills will get me closer to my career goal.	❏	❏
8. When I have a boring instructor, I realize I must work harder to make the material interesting.	❏	❏
9. My moods or personal problems seldom prevent me from completing my work.	❏	❏
10. I can visualize myself completing my goal.	❏	❏

CONTINUED

CONTINUED

Attitudes	Y	N
11. I know how to reward myself for finishing a difficult assignment.	❑	❑
12. I listen carefully while taking class notes, and I review them within 24 hours.	❑	❑

The results of this assessment will help you identify areas you need to focus on to improve your study habits. You can use this insight to create a plan to build effective study skills and achieve your learning goals.

Change Your Attitude: *Repeat this affirmation "I'm a strong, competent student." (From noted authority, Louise Hay) Write and repeat the affirmation over and over throughout the day. It will become a reality! I've used this affirmation for fifteen years, and it has changed my life for the better.*

Today's Diverse Classrooms

If you've been in school in recent years, you're already familiar with the diversity represented by today's students. If you haven't been in a classroom recently, you may find yourself in an environment more diverse than you previously experienced.

Diversity creates a rich learning environment where you benefit from the many life experiences of your classmates. You may encounter:

▶ People from various cultures, whose approach to personal development, school, teachers, and study is different from your own

▶ People who speak a variety of languages, who bring different communication patterns represented by their languages

▶ People of many ages learning together, encouraging the sharing of a wide variety of life experiences

▶ People who have various disabilities, who are now able to take part in classrooms in new ways thanks to technology and new types of learning aids

Available Help for Specific Needs

Because of the rapid growth of diversity in classrooms, schools now provide many kinds of assistance for students with special needs. If you're part of any of the groups above, if you're returning to school after several years away from the classroom, or if you have other concerns about studying successfully, take the time to explore and ask for the types of help you'd like to have. Speak to a teacher, a counselor, or an adviser.

Here are some examples of what's available:

▶ Study groups and tutoring for various learning styles

▶ ESL (English as a Second Language) classes, both as general language classes and as classes for specific study topics

▶ Assistance for students with physical disabilities, including modification of classroom equipment, several types of computer equipment, personal aides, readers, and note-takers

▶ Assistance for those with learning disabilities, including tutoring, study assistance for specific topics, and modification of learning materials and classroom procedures

Computers as Learning Tools

Throughout this book, you'll find suggestions for using a computer to help you study more effectively. But as you start looking at your approach to studying, it's important to be clear about what a computer can and can't do for you.

Computers Can	Computers Cannot
Help you take notes more quickly. Help you take online courses	Ensure that your notes will be more accurate
Help you file, organize, and store information	Replace thinking about what kind of organization you really need
Help you create papers that look organized, neat, and well-formatted	Take away the hard work of creating good content
Be a gateway to an enormous amount of information through Internet search engines	Replace the need to think carefully about the information you choose and use

How much you use a computer in the classroom and in your studying depends on several things: what your teacher requires, the specific subject you're studying, what resources you need for the subject, the equipment that's available to you, and how comfortable you are with using computers.

Have you been using a computer for years as a learning tool? Then remember that, as the topics you study become more advanced, you'll need to think more carefully and deeply about what you're learning, and you'll need to slow down to do that.

Are you going back to school and not accustomed to regular computer use? Often you'll have choices on how much or how little you use your computer as a learning tool. Some people still feel they do better with taking notes by hand, while others carry their laptops everywhere. Most teachers today expect that written assignments will be completed on a computer.

You can learn more about computer use in many ways. Talk with your teacher, advisor, or a reference librarian about what's available at your school. There are also many self-study books you can use; your teacher or adviser can help you choose what works for you.

Useful Websites: *Start with the main search engines, like Google, Yahoo, and so on. A list of current search engines can be found at www.wikipedia.com and www.philb.com.*

Your Focus Points

A definition of *accountability* is to be responsible for one's actions.

We all have good intentions. The thing that separates those who are successful from those who aren't is how well these good intentions are carried out.

Creating and putting in writing a specific plan can help convert your good intentions into action. Completing this exercise is a good starting point.

One important study skill is the ability to focus on what's important to you as you learn. Practice this skill now. Answer the following questions to help guide what you learn as you go through this book.

Note: *It's important for you to work through this entire book. This exercise will help you keep in mind your important focus points.*

FOCUS POINTS

1. Look back at the assessment you completed at the beginning of this part. List below the three things that you most want to focus on as you work through this book.

    a. _____

    b. _____

    c. _____

2. What motivates you to study?

    _____

    _____

3. Look back at the list you made about the specific needs you have for adaptations and help with learning. How, specifically, will you get those needs met.

    a. List the people you will go to for help with this. _____

    _____

    b. When do you plan to do this? _____

    _____

4. What's your Learning Style?

    a. **Visual:** Learn by seeing and reading.

    b. **Kinesthetic:** Learn by manipulating objects.

    c. **Auditory:** Learn by listening to lectures, tapes, and CDs.

Tip: *Use this awareness of your learning style to focus on how best to study and develop a learning strategy plan.*

The Getting Started Assessment

In this part, you:

1. Discovered your attitude toward learning.

2. Learned to use positive, present-tense affirmations, such as, "I'm a strong competent student," to improve your learning dramatically and, therefore, your grades.

3. Became aware that, in today's diverse classroom, there's support available for students with special needs and who need English as a Second Language.

4. Discovered that tutoring is available for most academic subjects and that peer counselors are assigned to study groups in some classes.

5. Explored how computers can be a help to you in many wonderful ways, but that they can't remove the need to create lucid and interesting writing.

6. Determined your Learning Style so you know how best to study using visual, kinesthetic, or auditory skills or some combination of all three.

Taking Control of

Your Time

If you don't know where you are going, you will probably end up somewhere else."

–Dr. Laurence J. Peter, American educator and author

In this part:

▶ Make Studying a Priority

▶ Say "Yes" to Dedicated Time

▶ Design a Study Schedule for You

▶ Choose What Is Most Important – Have Goals!

▶ Time Control: It's Your Choice!

Make Studying a Priority

Choosing specific times and places for study can be a difficult task, especially if you also have a job, are involved with family, or have other commitments. This section will help you look at where and when you study and give you some tips and strategies for making better use of time and place.

A Time—and Place—for Everything

How much time you spend studying, and where you do it, depends a lot on your individual situation. Which one of these is you? Check (√) or fill in those that apply.

- ❑   I am a full-time student.
- ❑   I am a full-time student, also working part-time.
- ❑   I am a part-time student, also working part-time.
- ❑   I am a part-time student, also working full-time.
- ❑   Other_____
- ❑   I have a private place for study.
- ❑   I have a shared space for study.
- ❑   I study wherever and whenever I can grab the chance.
- ❑   Other_____
- ❑   My study schedule affects other people close to me.
- ❑   I have these other commitments in my life:

_____

_____

_____

_____

Setting Goals

How do you balance all the aspects of your life and give priority to studying? Making clear choices, ranking priorities, and scheduling are the keys. Let's start by looking at time management.

Say "Yes" to Dedicated Time

Say yes to choices that support your commitment. If you have a choice, you may want to work fewer hours so that you can study more effectively. If you're working full-time and have other major commitments, you may be better off taking fewer courses spread over a longer time.

Say "yes" to dedicating some time to organize your time and place for study. You can save time later, if you spend time doing these things now.

Say "yes" to talking about your commitment to friends and family. This is especially important, if your choices will affect them in any way.

And Say "No" to Procrastination

You know that you want studying to be a priority. Most people don't have difficulty listing their priorities. The problem is learning when and where to say "No."

Learn to say "No" to extra demands on your time while you're studying. For example, if you're juggling work, study, and family, this may not be a good time to add volunteer work to your life.

Learn to say "No" to the voice inside your head that says "I'm too tired to study" or "Let's party." This doesn't mean school must be a boring or exhausting grind. It simply means that you learn to control your time to ensure that there's room for serious study and relaxation, as well as for other priorities in your life.

Learn to say "No" to multitasking while you're studying. It doesn't work, and it doesn't actually save time. You'll get more useful studying done if you put aside time for studying and nothing else. **Don't dread it! Do it!** Use affirmations that you create to avoid procrastination. Use the word "I" and the present tense, for example, "I don't dread it; I do it easily!"

Review the ideas on this page. Which ones are most important to you?

_____

_____

_____

What specific changes will you work on related to these ideas?

_____

_____

_____

Design a Study Schedule for You

Making choices is essential for academic success. And that applies to how you use your time. The following pages provide time-control tips, techniques, and strategies. By following these time-management tips, you'll be able to design your own flexible study schedule.

It's a good idea to follow your study schedule carefully for two or three weeks (making minor adjustments as needed) until it becomes routine. Remember, not all habits are bad; there are *good* habits, too! When you've written a goal, start by practicing it for 10 minutes. Don't condemn yourself for backsliding. Remember, a new habit takes at least 21 days of repetition to form.

The following exercise encourages you to:

- ▶ Set up monthly and yearly calendars and schedules for yourself

- ▶ Keep them where they're clearly visible

- ▶ Keep them where you can work with them easily

- ▶ Change old habits and create new ones

You can set up a study schedule on your computer, you can choose one of the many planning calendars or diaries that are available to buy, or you can create your own on paper—whichever works best for you.

Tip: **If you do set them up on your computer, be sure you have a disk or paper backup.**

HOW WELL ARE YOU USING YOUR TIME?

Read each question and answer it by checking either Yes (Y) or No (N). If you answer No to any of these questions, set a date to get started on those items.

Questions	Y	N	Date to Start
1. Do you have a large monthly calendar?	☐	☐	_____
Write all important tests, deadlines, and activities on a large monthly calendar. Place it in a conspicuous location. Use color to highlight important dates or events (such as exams).			
2. Do you have a weekly appointment calendar?	☐	☐	_____
Use one that shows a "week at a glance" and has space for daily scheduling, so you have a good overview of the entire week.			
3. Do you have a weekly study plan?	☐	☐	_____
Use a weekly study schedule to visualize and organize your time. Lightly pencil in your classes (by title on the days and times they meet) and block out times to eat, sleep, work, study, and relax.			
4. Do you plan for at least one hour of study for each class period?	☐	☐	_____
Protect time each day for study. With a regular schedule, your study time will soon become habit-forming.			
5. Do you plan for study breaks?	☐	☐	_____
Remember to limit your straight study time to no longer than one hour. It's important to take a 10-minute break between study periods to refresh yourself and give your mind a rest.			
6. Do you preview text assignments and review classroom notes from the previous class before your study time?	☐	☐	_____
Build this strategy into your weekly schedule. Note time for preview and review on your schedule.			

Study Skills Strategies

CONTINUED

Questions	Y	N	Date to Start

7. **Do you make effective use of any commute time to school each day (sometimes called dead time)?** ☐ ☐ _____

If you travel to class and have an opportunity to do some schoolwork, this is an ideal time to preview or review. Mark all commute time on your schedule.

8. **Do you leave sufficient time for relaxation and play?** ☐ ☐ _____

Play is therapeutic. Without it, you're only half a person. Make sure you have time for play noted on your calendar. You might also want to include relaxing activities, such as exercise and meditation.

9. **Do you reward yourself for meeting goals?** ☐ ☐ _____

Find small treats that are affordable or even free. (Don't accept your reward if you don't meet your goal!)

10. **Are you a list maker?** ☐ ☐ _____

It's a great idea to keep lists. Assign a priority to items on your list and complete the most important ones first. Carry forward items not completed to your next list. Do you make a list the night before? That's a strategy that highly effective people use.

Here's a chance to practice setting priorities. As you did this assessment, you probably noted several things you want to do or improve. Write your three top priorities and the dates you've chosen to start working on them.

First Goal: _____ Date to start: _____

Second Goal: _____ Date to start: _____

Third Goal: _____ Date to start: _____

Zig Ziglar, famous motivational speaker, says that the first step is to write down your goal along with start and end dates.

Choose What Is Most Important – Have Goals!

Setting priorities and writing them down is an important practice for good time management. If you don't already do this, start now. You can use the format here or any other format that works for you. This kind of list-making should become a habit.

If you already do this regularly, take a minute to think about it: Does your system work for you? If not, use the following sample form to play with new ideas for yourself.

If you aren't in the habit of ranking priorities, take a few minutes now to practice on the next page, listing your priorities for today (or tomorrow). Use the letters A, B, or C to note which ones are most important (the letter A representing the most important).

As you work on your priorities, remember that setting priorities means making choices, not trying to fit everything in. Make choices that say yes to some things and no to others.

Tip: *Be realistic. Plan to accomplish a few projects or errands each day. As you complete an item, check it off. You may need to change your expectations to increase your performance.*

Some goals are short-term and others are long-term. When adding a new habit, attach it to something you already routinely do.

TODAY'S PRIORITY LIST

Date: _____

Priority A, B, or C		School	Done
_____	1. _____		☐
_____	2. _____		☐
_____	3. _____		☐

Work

_____	1. _____		☐
_____	2. _____		☐
_____	3. _____		☐

Personal

_____	1. _____		☐
_____	2. _____		☐
_____	3. _____		☐

GOALS / AFFIRMATIONS

_____	1. _____		☐
_____	2. _____		☐
_____	3. _____		☐

Carry forward incomplete priorities
or affirmations to a new list for tomorrow.

Example of a Weekly Study Schedule

		MON	TUE	WED	THU	FRI	SAT	SUN
AM	6-7	Breakfast	Breakfast	Breakfast	Breakfast	Breakfast		
	7-8		Get Ready for School Review					
	8-9	History	Chem	History	Chem	History		
	9-10	Study	↓	Study	↓	Study		
	10-11	↓	Study	↓	Study	↓		Worship
	11-12	English	↓	English	↓	English		
PM	12-1	Lunch	Lunch	Lunch	Lunch	Lunch	Lunch	Lunch
	1-2	Work	Work	Work	Work	Work	Work	Study
	2-3	↓	↓	↓	↓	↓	↓	↓
	3-4	↓	↓	↓	↓	↓	↓	↓
	4-5	↓	↓	↓	↓	↓	↓	
	5-6	Study	Gym	Study	Gym			
	6-7	Dinner	Dinner	Dinner	Dinner	Dinner	Dinner	Dinner
	7-8	Study	Study	Study	Study			Study
	8-9	↓	↓	↓	↓			↓
	9-10							

Now turn to the blank weekly schedule on the next page and write in what would be a realistic schedule for you.

Tip: *Do this in pencil! You may want to change it again as you work on it or as you go through this book.*

After you have an idea of the kind of schedule that works for you, you can put it or something similar in whatever paper or computer form works best for you. Both part-time and full-time students can use this form.

WEEKLY SCHEDULE

		MON	TUE	WED	THU	FRI	SAT	SUN
AM	6-7							
	7-8							
	8-9							
	9-10							
	10-11							
	11-12							
PM	12-1							
	1-2							
	2-3							
	3-4							
	4-5							
	5-6							
	6-7							
	7-8							
	8-9							
	9-10							

1. When do you plan for the next day or week? _____

2. When do you review your notes from the previous week? _____

3. How many times a week do you review the text or notes for a class? _____

4. Do you record lectures (with the instructor's permission) and listen during your commute or when you're completing routine tasks? _____

YOUR STUDY SPACE

Answer the following questions. Use them to help you decide what you need to make your study space work better for you.

1. Do you have a private study space, such as your own room? Or do you share a space with someone else?

   _____

   _____

   _____

2. What kind of lighting does your study space have? Could you improve it? How? Does the light come over your shoulder?

   _____

   _____

   _____

3. Do you have plenty of space for your books, computer, and other study materials? Could you improve this space? How?

   _____

   _____

   _____

4. Do you have a chair and a writing space that helps you maintain good posture while you work? Could you improve that? How?

   _____

   _____

   _____

5. When you study away from your regular study space, do you choose spaces that allow you to concentrate well, if possible? What kinds of spaces might work better for you?

   _____

   _____

   _____

Time Control: It's Your Choice!

Here's a summary of the time-control tips in this section. Good time control is about making choices and setting goals that work for you. Review these tips and check (√) those that are most important for you to practice.

- ❑ Keep a written list of your priorities and goals and review them regularly for needed changes. Create affirmations that motivate you to maintain your mental energy.

- ❑ Create a schedule that supports your commitment to learning.

- ❑ Create a schedule that shows a realistic balance in your life.

- ❑ Talk with friends and family about your study needs and commitment.

- ❑ Create a monthly schedule that shows all major activities for the month.

- ❑ Create a weekly schedule that shows specific times for study and other activities.

- ❑ Look for added opportunities to study, such as commute times or between classes.

- ❑ Plan for preview and review times before and after classes (5-20 minutes).

- ❑ Arrange the place where you do most of your study so that it's well-lit, comfortable, and stocked with the resources and equipment you need.

- ❑ Reward yourself when you meet your goals.

Note-Taking

Techniques

There is no such thing as a worthless conversation, providing you know what to listen for. And questions are the breath of life for a conversation."

–James Nathan Miller, writer

In this part:

- ▶ Prepare for Effective Note-Taking
- ▶ Choose a Note-Taking Format
- ▶ Structured Note-Taking
- ▶ Informal Note-Taking
- ▶ Note-Taking by Computer
- ▶ The Keys: Listening and Participation
- ▶ Different Notes for Different Needs
- ▶ Improve Your Note-Taking Speed
- ▶ Taking Research Notes

Prepare for Effective Note-Taking

Note-taking is one of the most important things you do in class. It's your first step in working with the class material. When you take notes well, you're on your way to mastering the important information from each class.

Taking good notes starts with the way you approach the class. Here are some tips for preparing yourself:

1. Always read your assignment before you come to class. Doing so gives you background information and makes the lecture easier to understand. Be prepared!

2. Find a seat near the front of the room. Up close, you can see visual aids, be more aware of the instructor's facial expressions, hear better, and be less inclined to daydream.

3. Identify other serious students in each class and get to know them. Get their phone numbers in case you have questions or need help during the term.

4. Learn to listen for main ideas. Abbreviate, when possible. Don't try to write down everything the instructor says.

5. Learn to watch the instructor and copy everything he or she writes. This is especially true for examples, solutions, outlines, and definitions.

6. Organize and index your notes in a way that works for you. If you're allowed to use the notes on any exam, you'll be ahead of the game.

7. If you have difficulty taking notes because of any limitations you have, talk with your instructor or adviser. Most schools have assistance available or can help you find the resources you need.

8. Create an affirmation such as, "I am an excellent listener and note-taker."

The tips outlined on the next few pages will give you specific ideas on taking notes that work for you.

Choose a Note-Taking Format

There's more than one way to take notes effectively, beginning with choosing whether to write notes on paper or to use a computer. Then you can decide if you prefer to jot down important points informally or to structure your notes in a more formal outline style. The following case study illustrates these variations.

Tip: *The guidelines on this page are presented in outline format to refresh your memory on how to outline material. As you read, check (√) or highlight the tips that are important to you.*

I. **Choose and prepare your tools**

    A. If you use paper, keep your notes organized in a spiral or three-hole notebook.

        1. Avoid loose-leaf folders that allow pages to get lost.

        2. Don't forget extra pens or pencils!

    B. If you use a laptop, have software and folders set up so that you can start taking notes immediately in class.

II. **Set up your format**

    A. Review the sample notes that follow. Use one of these formats or experiment with something similar until you have a format you like.

    B. Date each lecture and number all pages for that course in sequence.

    C. Write recall words and abbreviations of main ideas in a margin or other specific place.

        1. Fill in recall words when you first review your notes.

        2. Leave room to write study questions on the same page or a facing page to assist you when you review.

    D. In your own words, summarize the main ideas in a specific place on the page (or write questions you need to ask your instructor).

    E. Use an outline rather than writing full paragraphs.

        1. Indent secondary ideas, supporting documentation, and examples.

        2. Always leave room when a new point is being developed.

        3. Use incomplete sentences or phrases. (Notice the phrases used on the samples.) Make sure you know the meaning of all your incomplete sentences.

Structured Note-Taking

This style organizes key ideas in outline form on the right-hand page and study notes on the left-hand page. The format is clear and simple to read. Its value is in stressing key points and important words that you can use later as a guide for more detailed study, perhaps from a textbook. Notice the space reserved for vocabulary and other information.

Study Notes & Questions
or Textbook Notes

What are 2 types of memory?

(1)

(2)

What are 3 memory tips?

(1)

(2)

(3)

Classroom Notes
Memorization Strategies

Feb 27th

Recall Cues
MEM?
LT
ST

1. Memory-Types of
   A. Long Term
   B. Short Term
2. Strategies
   A. Mnemonics
   B. Silly Sentences
   C. Visualization

STR?
Mne.
S. Sent.
Vis.

Use this space for:
1. Summary in your own words,
2. Questions, or
3. New vocabulary.

Compare this format to your own approach to note-taking.

Which note-taking ideas in this format might be helpful to you?

_____

_____

Some formats are better for specific class subjects. Would this type of format be useful for any subjects you're studying or plan to study? Which ones?

_____

_____

Informal Note-Taking

This format uses a different, less formal kind of outline. Notice that, although the notes may look less formal, they're still well-organized. Organization is key, no matter what your preferred style. Notice that the student in this example has made additional notes on studying and on what the teacher has stressed as important.

TOPIC: Memorization

Sept 27th

Two Types of MEM - difference important!
Long Term
Short Term
Check text for diff uses of each kind

MEM Strategies (look up words in text)
Mnemonics - use first letters
Silly sentences - fun to use
Visualization - see it any way that helps

Remember TEST on this chapter on Friday!
Vocabulary and examples imp!

Compare this format to your own approach to note-taking.

Which note-taking ideas in this format might be helpful to you?

_____

_____

Some formats are better for specific class subjects. Would this type of format be useful for any subjects you're studying or plan to study? Which ones?

_____

_____

Note-Taking by Computer

This example shows notes taken on a laptop. When taking notes on a computer, you can use a format similar to the two previous ones. Notice that this student has kept the formatting simple. Using fancy fonts or formats only wastes time. You can, however, take advantage of electronic features, such as underlining, bold, and highlighting, if you're comfortable using them quickly during a lecture. You can also set up organized folders and documents for each subject.

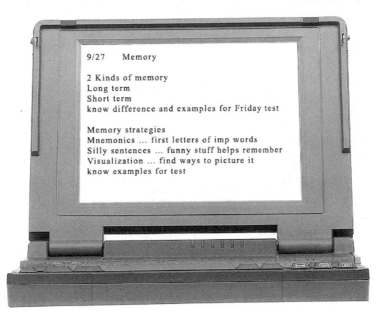

Compare this format to your own approach to note-taking.

Which note-taking ideas in this format might be helpful to you?

_____

_____

Some formats are better for specific class subjects. Would this type of format be useful for any subjects you're studying or plan to study? Which ones?

_____

_____

The Keys: Listening and Participation

Setting up your note-taking format is only the first step. After that comes the real work: focusing and getting all the important ideas and details. Listening and participation are your keys to effective note-taking and learning. Remember the affirmation, "I am an excellent listener and note-taker." You can develop your own affirmation, if you choose.

The following explains how to listen and participate in class with the added practice of being in outline form.

I. Listening

1. Stay focused on the teacher and listen for key ideas.

2. Listen for the following signals from your instructor about what's important:

    a. Voice changes usually indicate important points—listen for increases in volume or dramatic pauses.

    b. Repetition is a clue that an important point is being made.

    c. Gestures may indicate a major point.

3. Listen to and stay involved in all classroom discussions.

4. Ask questions, especially when things are unclear.

II. Taking Lecture Notes

1. What points should you note?

    a. Key ideas and main points

    b. All important terms and definitions

    c. Lists

    d. Formulas or solutions

2. Listen for secondary ideas. Indent or space so you can see that they're secondary.

3. Listen for connections and draw arrows to show connections between ideas.

4. Whenever you're in doubt, write it down. In discussion classes, jot notes on important points—particularly questions asked and conclusions reached during the discussion.

5. Spell new words as well as you can by the sound. Look up the correct spellings the first chance you get, or ask your instructor for help. If you're using a laptop, the spell checker might help.

6. Use symbols, diagrams, and drawings to illustrate ideas.

III. Participate in Class

Many teachers incorporate class participation into your grade.

Different Notes for Different Needs

You'll take better notes and get more out of your classes if you learn to adjust your note-taking to the type of class and the subject. Some classes are based on the discussion of ideas, while others are based on facts and definitions. Your teacher may be using lecture, discussion, visual aids, lab work, or any combination of these. Here are some added tips for taking notes in various situations.

As you read, place a check (√) near the tips that are important to you.

- ❑ When there's a lot of discussion in the class, note the questions and ideas that your classmates bring up, whether you agree with them or not. Note also the further questions and conclusions the teacher emphasizes.

- ❑ In a lab class, note the topic and the reason for the lab work. Note all the steps you take in the work, and if you have choices, why you picked the choices you made. Note any conclusions or results you come to.

- ❑ When the teacher uses various visual aids—from simple charts and posters to PowerPoint presentations and videos—note what points the teacher emphasizes with the visual aid. Take notes on all the key points that are illustrated. Ask if the visual aids will be available to you for study later.

- ❑ When the class involves a lot of factual, specific information—for example, a science or math class—note as much of the information as you can during the class. Add definitions or examples during the class, or note where you can get them later.

- ❑ **IMPORTANT!** Use your textbooks for added note-taking, whether you use them during the class period or not. Highlight and underline. Make notes in the margins. Use the table of contents and the index to help you find information.

- ❑ When you take an online class, you still need to take notes. As in any other class, use your notes to focus on main topics, important details, and the organization of ideas to help you study.

- ❑ If you have special needs related to note-taking, ask your teacher or adviser to help you with the adaptations or assistance you need.

Improve Your Note-Taking Speed

Whether you take notes by hand or use a computer, it helps to be able to note things quickly. Note-taking isn't the time for anything fancy or elaborate. Your goal is to get the information down.

Taking Notes by Hand

You can increase your writing speed by changing your handwriting.

REVIEWING YOUR HANDWRITING

In your normal handwriting, write the following sentence in the space below: "Note-taking isn't the time for anything fancy; just get the information down."

Observe the following writing sample that has excessive details. Notice how difficult the sample is to decipher. Now look at your sample (above). Does it have any excessive strokes or flourishes?

Note-taking is not the time for fancy writing.

Simplify your handwriting; some printing may be necessary.

Note-taking is the time to simplify. Change ∫ to I.

CHANGING YOUR HANDWRITING

Rewrite the following sentence in the space below: "Note-taking isn't the time for anything fancy; just get the information down." This time simplify your handwriting so that it's quick and easy to read.

_____

_____

Taking Notes Using a Computer

Use only one easy-to-read font, in a point size of at least 11 or 12, so you can clearly see what's on the screen as you type.

Leave spell-checking for later, except for important words related to the lesson.

If you'd like to improve or speed up your keyboarding, a number of programs are available. Check your school bookstore or your favorite office supply or computer store.

Recommended Reading: *For an excellent book on learning to type using the touch-typing method, go to www.axzopress.com and search for the Crisp series title, KAZ (Keyboarding A-Z).*

Review Immediately!

Whenever possible, spend five to 20 minutes reviewing your notes immediately after class or as soon as you can. Fill in missing areas and rewrite garbled notes. Studies show that short periods of study improve long-term memory.

Use Note-Taking Abbreviations

Abbreviate, omit, invent, and simplify in any way that helps you. Just remember that you'll have to read and understand the notes afterwards! Be sure that you use abbreviations that work for you.

EXAMPLES OF NOTE-TAKING ABBREVIATIONS			
>	increase	=	equals, is
<	decrease	ex.	example
→	caused, led to	def.	definition
w/ w/o	with, without	i.e.	that is
≠	doesn't equal, isn't	vs.	versus
sig.	significant	bec.	because
imp.	Important	esp.	especially

Text-Messaging Abbreviations

Text messaging has created a new way of abbreviating words—for example, using IC for "I see," RU for "Are you?," and 4U for "for you." If you're familiar with text-messaging language, then put it to work for you when you take notes, whether you take notes by hand or on your laptop. Text messaging is designed to put as much information as possible into as few characters as possible, so it's ideal for note-taking.

Do you use other types of abbreviations or text messaging? Add your own below:

_____

_____

_____

Taking Research Notes

When you're doing research as added study, as part of writing a presentation, or for a paper, use the same skills as for taking class notes. Pay attention to main points, look for subordinate ideas, and organize your notes so you can use them later.

Take and sort your notes by topic. If you just write bits of information one after another on the same page, you'll have a lot of hard work ahead of you when you start using such notes. Use a method that allows you to separate notes by topic as you go along.

Improve Your Research Skills

Whether you use a library, online search, or other resources, learn how to focus your research so you can get what you need without wasting a lot of time. Jot down ahead of time your general subject and some of the specifics you might be looking for. Create a question that you're trying to answer to help you develop a thesis statement (the main idea of a paper or presentation).

Librarians can help you get started and show you how to use library resources. Most libraries now have online catalogs, so you can look for material you might want to use even before you go to the library. Some schools have classes on how to do research; take advantage of them, if you can.

For doing online research, learn to do specific and advanced searches. Most search engines have directions for doing this. Otherwise, you'll be faced with far more information than you could ever use. Also, be sure that any information you find is accurately related to what you're doing. Similar words and phrases can bring up Web sites that look like what you want but aren't actually related to your topic.

Taking Research Notes by Hand

If you take research notes by hand, the tried and true method of using index cards—one card for each item of information—is still the best way to go. Each time you find information you can use, write it on a card. Use quotation marks when it's a direct quotation. Otherwise, put it in your own words.

At the top of the card, write the topic it relates to. Below the information, write where you got it: the author, the book or publication, the page number, the publisher, the publication date, and any other important information. Prepare one bibliography card with these details.

When you're ready to start writing, it's easy to sort out your cards by topic and line them up the way you'll use the information in your work.

Taking Research Notes by Computer

Look back at the ideas above for taking notes by hand. You want to accomplish the same thing—notes that are separate and easy to sort by topic. You also want to have the same information: notes, topic, source. Some software programs have note features that simulate separate index cards. You can also do something like this with any word processing program: set up a separate page for each topic and put all the information that relates to that topic on the page that you've set up for it.

When you're ready to start writing, you can easily organize your notes further using the features that allow you to move text around.

Your Notes Are Not Your Paper

Always—*always!*—write your own paper or presentation from your notes and research sources. Your notes are just the beginning. They're the information you'll use to create your own work; they're support for your work.

Always—*always!*—credit your sources. Tempting as it is, especially with the ease of finding information on the Internet and creating cut-and-paste documents on a computer, never use someone else's work and pass it off as your own. Follow the instructions your teacher gives you for noting sources as you write your paper.

Review and Focus

Here are the key points and tips for note-taking covered in this section.

▶ Prepare yourself for each class by doing assignments and reading before the class. Make marginal notations and highlight, underline, and number important information.

▶ Use note-taking tools that work for you: notebooks, binders, or your computer.

▶ Set up a system for note-taking. Include the date, the topic, and an organized way of setting up your notes on the page.

▶ In class, listen for main ideas, subtopics, and all the important facts.

▶ Take an active part in class. It helps you to learn more and to pay attention for good note-taking.

▶ Use handwriting or keyboarding techniques, such as abbreviations or text-messaging symbols, that allow you to take notes quickly.

▶ Adapt your note-taking to the kind of class you're in. Different subjects and different kinds of classes require specific kinds of notes.

▶ Request help with various types of adaptations if you need them for any challenge you face.

▶ Review your notes as soon as possible after class (within 5-20 minutes) to fill in any added information or to rewrite something that isn't clear.

▶ When you take notes for research, set up your notes so that you can easily sort and organize them.

▶ When you take notes for research, include the information, the topic, and the source. Put quotations around directly quoted material.

▶ Always credit your sources when you use information or work from someone else.

DEVELOPING YOUR STUDY SKILLS

Use these lines to write the points that you want to focus on as you develop your study skills:

_____

_____

_____

_____

_____

_____

Critical Reading

Skills

> *Language is the soul of the intellect, and reading is the essential process by which that intellect is cultivated beyond the commonplace experiences of everyday life."*

> **–Charles Scribner Jr., publisher**

In this part:

Reading: Your Key to Better Learning

Effective reading is probably the most important element of becoming an excellent student. If you can read well, you will:

▶ Get more out of your classes and your textbooks

▶ Be able to complete your reading assignments more easily

▶ Understand more clearly what you read

▶ Be able to pick out the essential information you need for assignments and research

With strong reading skills, you can help yourself learn. Unfortunately, not everyone is gifted with good reading ability. Like any other skill, however, reading can be developed and improved with practice.

Five Steps to Better Reading

In the pages ahead, you'll learn a five-step reading strategy to help you improve your reading skills. The strategy is called SQ3R. The five steps of this strategy will show you how to become a more critical reader—how to think carefully while you read.

You'll find that, whether you're taking notes, attending class, or reading, your goals are similar. **You want to focus on the main ideas, sort out the subtopics, and find the important details.**

Do You Need Extra Help?

For many reasons, some people need extra help with reading skills. Perhaps English is your second language. Or maybe you know that you've never really learned to read in any kind of detail, and you feel that you just barely get by with basic reading. You're not alone—many people need some added help with reading, and that's why schools and libraries have all kinds of help available. Talk with your teacher, your adviser, or a librarian. Don't be afraid to ask. By getting help, you're showing how much learning means to you.

SQ3R for Success

When you read a novel you like, you can move right along enjoying yourself. When you read a love letter, you savor each word and have absolutely no difficulty concentrating. You don't need to underline the main ideas or make marginal notes.

Textbook reading is different. You must learn to apply special reading and marking skills when you study complicated materials. The SQ3R reading technique (explained below) can reduce your study time and significantly increase your ability to grasp essential information.

Overview of SQ3R

The name SQ3R will help you remember the five steps in the process:

Step 1: Survey

Step 2: Question

Step 3: Read—and underline

Step 4: Recite—and write

Step 5: Review

If you've already learned this process, it may not have included underlining and writing in Steps 3 and 4. They're added here because they're important when you're reading to learn something specific.

Reading Material Online

If you read material on line or for a distance education class, use the same process. Take notes by hand as you read—you'll probably not be able to highlight, underline, or write notes in the margin of the material. Use the five steps to guide your notes.

SQ3R Step 1: Survey

Spend no more than 10 minutes to survey what you're going to read. This is like taking a sneak preview of the reading you've been assigned. You may not be in the habit of previewing and will consciously have to force this important first step.

Surveying for an Overview

Previewing provides an overview of the way the book, chapter, or reading assignment is organized. Smart travelers use a road map, and smart students survey first. You're making your own road map to follow as you read.

When you survey, do the following:

- ▶ Examine the title of each chapter.

- ▶ Note headings and subheadings and their relationship in each chapter.

- ▶ Glance at diagrams, graphs, and visuals.

- ▶ Quickly skim the introductory and concluding sections of each chapter.

- ▶ Notice any study questions or activities at the end of the chapter.

If you're reading on line, make some quick notes for yourself as you survey.

As you read this book, you can see how this works. Take a minute or two to look ahead and skim through the next part. Look at the headings and subheadings. Glance at the exercises. Don't read—just survey to see what the part is about.

After you've surveyed what you're going to read, you're ready to move on to the next step.

SQ3R Step 2: Question

Your next step is to see each part of what you read as the answer to a question. These questions will help you focus on what's important. For example, the first page of this section focuses on three questions:

▶ Why are reading skills important for learning?

▶ What is SQ3R?

▶ How do you get help with reading, if you need it?

When you question, you help yourself understand more of what you're reading, and you prepare yourself to focus on and remember the important points.

Begin with the first section of a chapter. Always read with the intent to answer a question. Use the words who, what, when, where, why, and how to help you turn each heading into a question.

If you are reading online or for an online class, write down the questions you use.

SQ3R PRACTICE 1

See if you can do this with what you've just read for Step 1 and Step 2 of SQ3R:

Two questions for Step 1:

1 _____

_____

2. _____

_____

Two questions for Step 2:

1. _____

_____

2. _____

_____

*Compare your answers with the author's suggested responses
in the Appendix.*

SQ3R Step 3: Read and Underline

Read each section with the question you developed in mind. After reading the section, go back to the beginning and underline, highlight, or mark the material using the techniques on this page and the next.

Read carefully and take your time. Speed reading techniques shouldn't be used for technical material, because important details may be missed. Don't be afraid to move your lips or read aloud. It's a myth that rereading a sentence is harmful. Critical reading may require you to reread items several times to understand a sentence or passage completely.

Tip: *Use a pen instead of a pencil, because pencil fades. If you prefer, use a highlighter. You could apply different colors for different kinds of information.*

If you read on line or for an online class, you can mark items if the software or program you're using allows you to do that. If it doesn't, make brief written notes on paper for yourself as you go along.

Suggestions for Marking

There are a lot of ways to mark what you read. Study these suggestions and adapt them so that they work for you.

Underline after reading

Read a paragraph or a section of the text and then go back and underline only the main points. Don't underline the first time you read the material. When you first read, read for understanding, not trying to memorize at that time.

Use Numbers

Write numbers to help you focus on a series of details. Use numbers for:

1. lists
2. enumerations
3. sequences

Vertical Line

Place vertical lines in the margin, like the line you see here, to emphasize main points that include several lines of text.

Asterisks

Use asterisks to signal *main points* and for other important points or ideas.

Recall Phrases

Place recall phrases in the margins to condense major points and provide supporting details. Summaries and questions may also be placed in the margins.

Definitions and Examples

Underline all definitions. Write "def" in the margin. Put parentheses ( ) around examples. If you underline or highlight the entire example, nothing will stand out, and your purpose for marking will be lost.

Circles or Boxes

Some students like to circle important concepts, ideas, or subheadings. Other students prefer a box.

Highlighting

Highlight the points underlined or highlight instead of underlining. Use a felt-tip pen. Yellow is often preferred. For online reading, some software programs include a highlighting feature.

??!!

React to what you read. Agree, disagree! Question? Stay involved with the ideas in the text! Show your reactions with any kind of punctuation or other mark that works for you.

SQ3R Step 4: Recite and Write

Once you've formed questions on your reading and have read to answer those questions, you're ready to recite the answers. Use your underlining and markings to guide you. Reciting helps you learn and remember what you've read. Don't skip this step, even if you think you know the information. This step will make a big difference in how well you master the material.

Recite the answers out loud (or quietly to yourself). Also, write brief study notes, which will help encode the information in your long-term memory for easier retrieval on the final examination.

Write a sentence summary of the main idea in each paragraph, if the material is extremely difficult for you.

The recall cues you wrote in the margins are an essential step. If you use those cues to recite, you may not need study notes for some classes.

IN YOUR OWN WORDS

Summarize the previous Step 4 recitation ideas in your own words.

_____

_____

_____

_____

_____

SQ3R PRACTICE 2

This practice puts together several of the SQ3R steps.

1. Start by writing two questions for the information you read above.

   Question one: _____

   _____

   _____

   _____

   Question two: _____

   _____

   _____

   _____

2. Go back over what you read above and mark it—underline or highlight and list some recall phrases.

3. Write the answers to the two questions you made up for this reading.

   Answer to question one: _____

   _____

   _____

   _____

   Answer to question two: _____

   _____

   _____

   _____

4. Do your questions, markings, and answers all work together for you?

*Compare your answers with the author's suggested responses
in the Appendix.*

SQ3R Step 5: Review

Once you've read an entire chapter, section by section, you're ready to review that chapter.

This is the final step in understanding the material.

1. Reread each main heading.

2. Review the underlined and highlighted material.

3. Answer the questions you formed for each section. Use your reading notes to help you review.

Practice reviewing with this book. Take a few minutes to go back through the pages of this part, reviewing the main headings and the work you did.

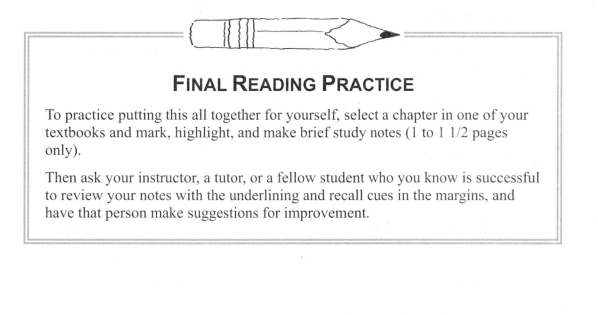

FINAL READING PRACTICE

To practice putting this all together for yourself, select a chapter in one of your textbooks and mark, highlight, and make brief study notes (1 to 1 1/2 pages only).

Then ask your instructor, a tutor, or a fellow student who you know is successful to review your notes with the underlining and recall cues in the margins, and have that person make suggestions for improvement.

A Lifetime Habit: Careful Reading

Whatever your age, it's important to make a habit of reading. You're never too young or too old to make reading an important part of your life. Reading for pleasure is as important as critical reading for learning.

As you study and plan for further learning, compile a list of books that would be helpful in meeting your goals. Ask teachers, librarians, and fellow students for ideas. Some teachers provide lists of suggested reading beyond actual assignments—always try to include at least one or two of them in your study plan. The earlier in your academic career you begin reading, the better.

Begin reading newspapers, magazines, and online material regularly and build your vocabulary as you go along. Oprah Winfrey has said that her stern father had her learn 20 new words and write one book report a week. Her grandmother taught her to read at 2 years old. We can't all be like Oprah, but we can begin to improve our reading skills at any age—and enjoy the process!

Tip: **This book includes a list of suggestions for further reading in the Appendix. Take a moment to look at it now. Ask your teacher or librarian for a list of books for college-bound students.**

Your Focus Points

Do you feel that you know a lot about what you read in this part?

You probably do—because you used SQ3R to learn SQ3R. As you read and did the exercises, you probably noticed that everything in this part gave you practice in the SQ3R method.

As you can see from your work in this part, it's a process that works. Try it with all your reading assignments. It's a valuable reading tool that, with practice, will become a habit you can use all your life.

DEVELOPING YOUR READING SKILLS

Reflect on what you learned by answering these questions, using the lines provided.

1. What ideas and suggestions were the most important for you in this part?

_____

_____

_____

_____

_____

2. Which suggestions do you want to focus on and practice more?

_____

_____

_____

_____

_____

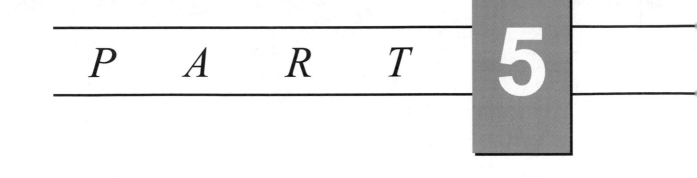

Memory Training

> ❝ *If we would have new knowledge, we must get a whole world of new questions.* ❞
>
> **–Susanne K. Langer, philosopher**

In this part:

Improve Your Memory

Human beings are capable of extraordinary feats of memory. In fact, experts in the study of memory agree that the skill isn't all due o an inborn ability but is developed through the use of various techniques and considerable practice.

Overcoming Memory Problems

Have you studied for hours trying to memorize material for a test and then gone blank? Practicing the memory strategies in this section will help you reduce blanking out.

But if your memory-related problems seem severe, if you have difficulty focusing your attention, if you have severe test-taking anxiety, or if you feel you may have a learning disability, talk with your counselor or instructor. A wide variety of helpful methods and treatment options are available today. Don't hesitate—getting help if you need it will remove obstacles so you can concentrate on being a successful student.

Switch to "Single-Tasking"

While you're studying and memorizing, avoid multitasking. Give your work your complete attention. Many studies have shown that multitasking doesn't speed up work; it only distracts you and slows you down.

Listening to music does help some people concentrate, but be sure that's true for you and that listening to music while you're learning isn't just a habit you've acquired. Chewing gum may help you focus and do better on math problems by 3% according to a Baylor University research study (2009).

Turn off TV, radio, cell phones, and any other interruptions—electronic or otherwise. If you're working at a computer, have only your study material on your screen. Single-tasking will pay off for you in easier and more effective learning.

Memory-Training Strategies

Like the experts, you too can improve your memory. In the next few pages, you'll learn eight study strategies that, if you understand and practice them, can make your studying not only easier, but more rewarding. As you go along, think about which ones will work best for you or about new ones you'd like to try.

These are the eight strategies:

1. Spread your memory work over several sessions

2. Recite material out loud to a partner or study group

3. Expect to remember (assume a positive attitude)

4. Organize your material into a meaningful pattern

5. Test and retest yourself—alone or with a study group

6. Over-learn

7. Use hooks, catchwords, and rhyming phrases or sentences

8. Study before sleeping

Let's take a look at each of these strategies in more detail.

Tip: *Research on Reversing Cognitive Decline.*

1. *Most importantly, exercise improves memory 20-30% by increasing blood flow to the brain.*

2. *Social ties, creative arts, and crossword puzzles help memory. Computer games may improve declining memory by 10 years, but the research findings are still insufficient in this area.*

Strategy #1: Spread Out Memory Work

Sometimes students think that the longer they study, the more they'll learn. Unfortunately, the reverse is true. Shorter periods of memory work, not more than two hours each, are far superior to six hours of frantic cramming.

Tip: *Reviewing memory work within 24 hours of the first study session is the most effective way to master the material.*

Distributed Practice

Probably the more time you spend studying, the better, but practice is the optimum strategy. An ideal learning pattern would involve:

1. Immediate review within the short-term memory span

2. A review after the first hour

3. A short review after overnight sleeping

4. A short review after a week

5. A short review after a month

Do you know how much more you'll be able to recall if you follow this schedule? Up to **88% of the material** you review will be saved in your long-term memory.

Strategy #2: Recite Material Aloud

When you're studying or memorizing, recite the answers to your study questions aloud so that you can hear the answer. Don't simply recite the answer in your head! That's a beginning, but only a beginning. Use a study group, study partner, or a tape recorder to help.

Question yourself aloud and answer yourself aloud.

If you study in a group or with a friend, quizzing each other will improve recall. Although your memory may begin to fail on a test, the voice of the person you studied with will often come through loudly and clearly.

Tip: **Research studies show that answering questions aloud improves recall by at least 80%!**

Use All Your Senses

The more senses you involve in the learning process, the longer you'll remember.

▶ **See It.** Read and visualize the material.

▶ **Say It.** Answer the questions aloud that you formulate from your class notes. Use your notes and the cues in the recall column of your textbook to help you ask yourself study questions.

▶ **Write It.** Write answers to questions from your study notes. Outline major points from the text.

▶ **Repeat It.** Repeat this entire process until you've mastered the material.

▶ **Smell It.** Associate a particular smell with what you're learning—for example, smells from a science laboratory or a pleasant scent you place nearby while studying.

Tip: **Create a song and sing it. Rhyming helps long-term recall.**

Strategy #3: Expect to Remember

Decide to remember! As obvious as this seems, many students fail to realize the power of intent to recall. Because you want to remember words to a favorite song, you can easily repeat the lyrics word for word.

It's amazing how much we're capable of remembering. Think about how many passwords, phone numbers, email addresses, and directions to people's homes that you remember. We remember these things because we want to do so. It's easier to remember them than to look them up each time.

If you *want* to remember, you will. Your attitude is the secret. Believe in yourself and in your ability to learn. Remind yourself of your commitment to learning. Think of the many reasons that you're studying and why you want to remember the material you're studying—for tests, yes, but also as a part of your overall learning goals.

Tip: *Use a positive affirmation in the present tense, so it's more active, and use "I". For example, "I know I can remember" and "I remember easily."*

Strategy #4: Organize the Material

People who recall long lists of numbers often can do so because they've found a *pattern* or a *relationship*.

FIND A PATTERN

Look at this string of numbers and take a moment to try to memorize the list.

3   6   9   12   15   18   21

What's the pattern in this string of numbers? Write your answer below.

_____

_____

Compare your answer with the author's in the Appendix.

Learning this set of numbers was easier for you if you recognized the pattern. The same is true about anything you need to remember. Break up the material into some kind of pattern.

You did this in another way when you learned and practiced SQ3R. When you read material with the SQ3R method, your markings become a pattern that helps you organize and remember the material.

Tip: *Include no more than seven chunks of information in each organizational pattern. Cognitive psychologists have found that we best retain a maximum of <u>seven chunks of information</u>. Telephone numbers (excluding area codes) are examples of the need to limit information to seven bits for better recall.*

Strategy #5: Test and Retest

If you had to learn 10 definitions for class tomorrow, how could you test yourself? Would you write the definitions over and over or read the list aloud 20 times? Neither method is the best choice.

Instead, follow this self-testing process:

1. Memorize the *first* item.

2. Go on to the *second* item and memorize it.

3. Now repeat the first item *and* the second by memory.

4. When you know those two, go on to the *third*.

5. Memorize the third item *and* repeat items one, two, and three.

6. Continue in this same manner until you have learned all 10 definitions.

Tip: Don't forget to use all your senses!

TESTING YOUR MEMORY SKILLS

1. Go back to Strategy #3, Expect to Remember.

   a. Affirm the statement from The Little Engine that Could, "I think I can, I think I can, I know I can, I know I can, I knew I could, I knew I could."

   b. Memorize something about it that's important to you and will help you study.

   c. After you've learned it, close the book for a moment and say it from memory.

2. Move on to Strategy #4, Organize the Material.

   a. Again, memorize something about this that's helpful and important to you.

   b. After you've learned it, close the book and recite both items you've learned, the one from Strategy #3 and the one from Strategy #4.

3. Now memorize something helpful to you from Strategy #5, Test and Retest. Got it? Close the book again, and recite and write all three items to yourself.

   a. _____

   b. _____

   c. _____

Strategy #6: Over-Learn

Review material that you've learned several times. When final examinations or midterms come around, you will have mastered material that you've encoded for long-term recall. In math classes, rework the model or sample five or more times to encode the correct formula into your long-term memory.

Commercials can haunt you for years because of the repetition of a jingle or song. You've over-learned them, simply because you've heard and sung them so often— even when you didn't want to. You get the same effect when you review and recite material again and again.

Over-learning can give you confidence when you're working with material that's difficult for you. As you work with it over and over, it will become familiar to you and you'll be able to recall it more easily.

THINK ABOUT IT

1. Can you think of a commercial, or a saying, or something else that you know you'll remember because you over-learned it? Write it here.

_____

_____

_____

_____

_____

2. Where would over-learning be helpful for you in the subjects you're studying?

_____

_____

_____

_____

_____

Strategy #7: Use Recall Hooks

Create hooks and catchwords that help you recall what you're memorizing. You've already seen one of them in this book: SQ3R is a hook that helps you remember the five steps of reading effectively.

You hook the idea into your memory bank by using mnemonic phrases or catchwords to pull up more information and recall the details. For example, some people use ROY G. BIV to remember the colors of the rainbow.

Red **O**range **Y**ellow   **G**reen   **B**lue **I**ndigo **V**iolet

Making Up Catchwords

You can create your own catchwords to go with whatever you're learning. Students working together often have fun doing this. For example, to remember the eight memory strategies in this section, you can employ a similar hooking device.

R   **R**ecall with hooks and catchwords

O   **O**rganize the material

O   **O**ver-learn

S   **S**pread out memory work

T   **T**est and retest

E   **E**xpect to remember

R   **R**ecite aloud

S   **S**tudy before sleeping and upon awakening

If the order isn't important, you can create a catchword or phrase from the first letter of the words. The strange or bizarre is usually easier to remember.

Rhyming

If words must be remembered in a specific order, then a rhyming nonsensical sentence may help you remember. Rhymes can help you remember many types of information. When rhythm is added, the results are even better. We all know -

> *Thirty days hath September,*
> *April, June and November;*
> *February has twenty eight alone*
> *All the rest have thirty-one*
> *Except in Leap Year, that's the time*
> *When February's Days are twenty-nine*

Notice that the poem rhymes and has rhythm. Some students like to borrow cheers from their school's sports teams and put in new words to help memorize things like mathematical formulas.

If English is your second language, do you know rhymes or poems in your first language that you can use to help you remember what you learn? If so, go ahead and use them, as long as you know how to translate the information into English when you take a test. Using our first language can help us think in different ways about something. You might even have some fun sharing your rhymes with other students!

Strategy #8: Study Before and After Sleep

To get the most mileage from study and memory work, try to review right before going to sleep. Cut off the television and don't become otherwise distracted.

You'll process this new material while you're sleeping. As you wake, review again. To put a tight cap on the bottle of information you're encoding for future recall, review again later the same morning.

Also, pay attention to what time of day is your best learning time. Although other obligations or activities may prevent you from studying at that time, try to do it whenever you can. If possible, change your study schedule sometimes to take advantage of your best study time.

MEMORY STRATEGIES

Write the acronym for 8 memory strategies.

R_____

O_____

O_____

S_____

T_____

E_____

R_____

S_____

Visualize for Success

Visualizing what you study is one of the most effective ways to remember just about anything. You've heard the saying, "A picture is worth a thousand words." Although you may not remember a thousand words with just one image, a picture is a powerful way to help yourself learn.

Use Images as Reminders

When you read about Strategy #7, Recall Hooks, you discovered the author's suggested catchword ROOSTERS. Each letter is a signal for the first word of one of the eight memory techniques.

If you want to remember even longer, *visualize* the catchword in your mind's eye or associate the word with an object or a place with which you're already familiar. Can you remember the image of roosters in a picture book from your childhood or, even better, actual roosters that you've seen? This is a strong image that you won't easily forget.

When you can visualize items from your text or classroom notes, they're much easier to recall. The rooster visualization is an example of how to use association to remember. Simpler visual displays can be just as effective.

Use Graphics as Reminders

Another powerful technique for recalling information is to distill it into a graphic or visual display. This technique forces you to analyze the information and arrange it in a non-textual manner. Understanding the interrelationships of data makes it easier to remember. Study the following pages for examples of graphical displays you can use to organize information and improve your recall.

Tip: *Association is an important technique for efficient recall.*

Sample Graphics

You can use graphics such as these when you take notes in class, as you organize your resources for study, and when you want to memorize specific material. If you use your computer for studying, you can use any features you're comfortable with to create visual aids on your computer. (Just don't get so absorbed in creating graphics that you lose valuable study time.)

Chronological Timelines

These are useful for history classes or any subject that includes time periods. College bookstores and other bookstores often have prepared timelines for study aids.

Tree Diagrams

These are popular among biology students and genealogists, but the image can be used for many academic subjects.

TREE MAP

Try listing five skills you've learned from this section. Fill in this tree map using the five memory strategies (from the previous pages) that are most important to you.

1. _____

2. _____

3. _____

4. _____

5. _____

Flow Chart

Flow charts are helpful for math, project management, or any subject matter that includes a sequence of steps.

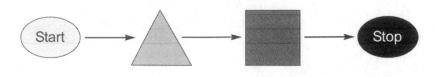

Study Map

Use a study map to show how various points relate to a main topic. This method is especially helpful for subjects like management, social studies, or others that include discussion of ideas or that require you to organize your thinking around a specific concept.

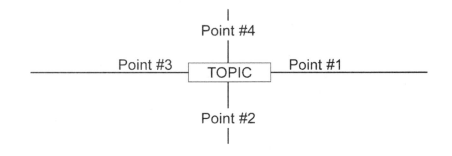

Sun Shapes or Clocks

Patterns like these help you remember sequences, particularly sequences that run in cycles. Examples are economic cycles, business cycles, and life cycles.

Clustering or Branching Lines

These are useful for grouping ideas when you need to remember them to present in an organized way, such as an essay exam or a class presentation.

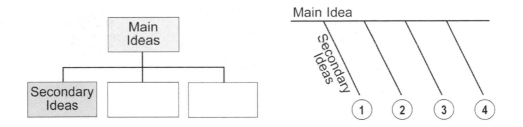

Hand Prints

Hand prints are a simple visual you can use for any topic when you need to remember ideas or concepts of equal importance. You can also use this device when you're giving a speech. Visualize a key word on each finger.

Loci Method

The ancient Greeks used the rooms of a house (*loci* is Latin for "locations") to help remember the points of a speech. You can do the same by walking through the front door and visualizing your introduction, moving into the living room for your first point, and so on.

The point is that we can link new information more easily onto a previous memory, like our homes or even parts of our cars. Use whatever is the most vivid and familiar "memory structure" for you as you apply the loci method.

Tip: *Color helps! It creates stronger "glue" for your mind and is highly recommended by cognitive psychologists. It's also sometimes more fun!*

Review of Memory Techniques

The Eight Memory Strategies

1. Spread memory work over several sessions

2. Recite material out loud

3. Expect to remember (assume a positive attitude and use affirmations)

4. Organize the material into a meaningful pattern

5. Test and retest yourself

6. Over-learn

7. Recall: use hooks, catchwords, and rhyming

8. Study before sleeping and upon awakening

Visualize for Success

▶ Use chronological timelines to remember dates

▶ Sketch trees and fill in the branches with material to be learned

▶ Use flow charts to remember a sequence

▶ Create a study map

▶ Make sun shapes or clocks to remember the relation of various items

▶ Cluster thoughts in an outline format

▶ When there are 10 or fewer items to learn, use hand prints

▶ Use the loci method

Tip: **Review this section of study skills strategies often.**

BUILDING YOUR MEMORY SKILLS

On the lines below, list the three ideas about memory that you want to work on to build your learning skills.

Exam Strategies

To be able to be caught up into the world of thought—that is to be educated."

–Edith Hamilton, educator, writer, and historian

In this part:

Taking Tests Well

Kayla was a typical student who faced a common challenge—three major tests and a final examination would account for 60% of her final grade. Often Kayla blanked out on exams and found it difficult to finish during the time allotted. If you've felt this test-taking anxiety, you're not alone.

Successful students learn sound strategies for taking tests. After you have a good understanding of taking classroom notes, reading your textbook, and memory training, you're ready to "score" by learning test-taking strategies.

Relaxation tapes and techniques can also reduce stress and be an enormous help to you. Relaxation is crucial for optimal learning, so try a few deep breaths before you begin to study or as you start a test. Some researchers have found that playing Baroque music is particularly helpful for learning at home or in the classroom. If Baroque music doesn't appeal to you, try something soothing and calming. This creates a linkage between the right and left brain and establishes an emotive link with the material.

LEFT BRAIN emphasizes:

language

mathematical formulae

logic

numbers

sequence

linearity

analysis

words of a song

HUMAN BRAIN

RIGHT BRAIN emphasizes:

forms and patterns

special manipulation

rhythm and musical appreciation

images/pictures

imagination

daydreaming

dimension

tune of a song

Mastering Objective Tests

To do well on an objective test, you need to memorize facts and thoroughly understand concepts and relationships. The following hints should help you score higher on true-false and matching type questions. Use your instructor as a resource. Ask what type of questions will be on the test, and then prepare accordingly.

Note: *Use the same tips when you're taking tests on line. If your instructor permits, have pencil and paper with you to write down key words or work out possible answers.*

Some Hints:

▶ **Look over the entire test.** Know how much each question is worth, and budget your time accordingly. Check the clock every 10 minutes to ensure that you won't be caught off guard and run out of time. If necessary, put your watch on the desk in front of you.

▶ **Answer the easiest questions first.** Put a check by those that are harder and return to those questions last. Otherwise, you'll waste valuable time and miss answering the easier questions. Place another line through the check when you complete the harder questions.

▶ **Underline key words in the question.** Make special note of negative words like *not*. Feel free, however, to ask for clarification from your instructor if the question is vague or unclear.

Matching Questions

Approach matching-question testing as a game and play by the rules.

Rule # 1   As always, begin by reading the question and underlining or numbering key words.

Rule # 2   Glance over both columns quickly. Which column has the longer entries? Begin looking at that side so you can save time as you scan the shorter column for an answer each time.

Rule # 3   Warning! Don't select an answer unless you're certain you've selected a correct match. Why? Because you've substantially reduced the number of items left for the more difficult final matches.

Rule # 4   Circle or draw a line through each answer that you eliminate.

Rule # 5   As you eliminate the matches you're sure of, use your best guess for the correct answer. It's okay to guess at this point.

True-False Questions

▶ Answers containing such words as *all*, *never*, *always*, and *everyone* usually are wrong.

▶ On the other hand, qualifiers such as *frequently*, *probably*, and *generally* more often indicate a true answer.

Example

T   F   Class notes should *always* be rewritten.

The word *always* is a clue that the answer may be false.

Multiple-Choice Questions

1. Draw a line through each answer that you eliminate. (See example below.)

2. Ensure that the grammatical structure of the question agrees with your choice.

3. Read all choices. Even if the first answer seems correct, another choice may be better, or "all of the above" may be the correct response.

4. If you're at a complete loss, and there's no penalty for guessing, choose the longest answer—especially on teacher-made exams.

5. When opposite statements appear in a question, one of the statements is often correct.

Example

When two opposite statements appear in a multiple-choice question:

    a.   one of the opposite statements is usually correct.

    b.   ~~neither are correct~~.

    c.   ~~both are correct~~.

    d.   ~~choice in the middle is often correct~~.

Excelling on Essay Exams

Do essay exams create more anxiety for you than objective exams? Fear of unknown essay questions can be substantially reduced if you follow these six simple steps:

1. Use this basic guide to essay writing and other tests. It's an excellent Internet site. http://lklivingston.tripod.com/essay/

2. Develop your own practice essay questions by looking over your lecture notes and textbook assignments and guessing what the instructor would select. Write a practice essay and read it out loud

3. Sketch out a variety of outline responses to 10 or more possible questions.

4. Memorize the outlines using catchphrases or mnemonic devices.

5. Practice writing an essay within a specific time constraint. This is especially helpful if you have difficulty completing your tests.

6. Write an affirmation such as, "I am a strong, confident writer."

Improving Specific Essay Skills

Besides using the above steps to review and prepare for essay tests, you can use the following skills to help you succeed on essay exams:

▶ Essay Skill #1: Budget Your Time

▶ Essay Skill #2: Analyze Key Words

▶ Essay Skill #3: Create an Outline

▶ Essay Skill #4: Focus Your Essay

▶ Essay Skill #5: Build Strong Paragraphs

▶ Essay Skill #6: Use Transition Words

Use these skills and suggestions whether you write your essay by hand or on a computer. When you use a computer, have pencil and paper with you if your instructor permits. Use them to sketch out and organize your ideas.

Note: **You can use these essay exam skills for writing any essay assignment, even when it's not on a test. Building these skills will help you think in a more organized way, strengthen your writing, and improve your study skills overall.**

Essay Skill #1: Budget Your Time

Take a few minutes to look over the entire test and budget your time accordingly. Are the required answers all of equal length, or will you have to write longer or shorter answers for some questions? Note in the margins about how many minutes you want to use for each answer.

Check to see if your instructor has noted how many points an answer is worth. For example, if one question is worth 30 points, you want to give yourself plenty of time to work with it. If a question is worth 5 points, you can leave it till later in the test.

As you skim through the test, if key words or ideas come to you, you can jot them in the margins. Don't stop to answer the question fully at this time.

Decide which questions to answer first. It's usually best to start with those you know well, because you can accumulate points that way. Be sure, however, that answering all the easier ones first won't take time away you need from questions that are worth more points.

Essay Skill #2: Analyze Key Words

As you work on each question, read it carefully and underline key words. Think about what the question is asking you to do. For example, if you're asked to <u>trace</u> the development of social reform in America, you need to describe the historical development of the subject. On the other hand, if you're asked to <u>criticize</u> or <u>critique</u> a poem or book, your instructor expects you to show the positive and negative points and support your ideas with evidence.

If you're using a computer to take your test, and you have blank paper available, you can jot down the key words for each question as you go along. Or, if the system you're using permits, you can highlight or underline on the screen. (Some test-taking systems don't permit the user to change or mark the questions in any way.)

Key Words to Learn

Here are some other key words that often appear in essay exams or assignments.

evaluate	prove	illustrate
analyze	relate	diagram
delineate	state	discuss
compare	justify	enumerate
describe	evaluate	illustrate

If you aren't familiar with these words, look them up in a dictionary. Then try the following matching exercise.

ESSAY EXAM MATCHING QUIZ

The following words are frequently used in essay examinations. Match the word to the appropriate definition.

Hint: Remember the suggestions for taking matching quizzes and use them for this quiz.

_____ 1. summarize   A. Show good reasons for

_____ 2. evaluate   B. Establish the truth of something by giving factual evidence or logical reasons

_____ 3. contrast   C. Use a word picture, a diagram, a chart, or a concrete example to clarify a point

_____ 4. explain   D. Talk over; consider from various points of view

_____ 5. describe   E. Make plain; give your meaning of; translate

_____ 6. define   F. Sum up; give the main points briefly

_____ 7. compare   G. Give an account of; tell about; give a word picture of

_____ 8. discuss   H. Make clear; interpret; make plain; tell how to do

_____ 9. criticize   I. Give the meaning of a word or concept; place it in the class to which it belongs, and set it off from other items

_____ 10. justify   J. Bring out points of similarity and points of difference

_____ 11. trace   K. Bring out the points of difference

_____ 12. interpret   L. Follow the course of; follow the trail of

_____ 13. prove   M. State your opinion of the correctness or merit of an item or issue

_____ 14. illustrate   N. Give the good points and the bad ones; appraise

Compare your answers with the author's suggested responses in the Appendix.

Essay Skill #3: Create an Outline

Before you start writing, create an informal outline of the main ideas and supporting details that you need to answer the question. You may feel that you don't have time for this, but taking a moment or two to create an outline will make it easier for you to answer the question. It will also help ensure that you cover all the important points.

Are you using a computer to write your test? Then create your outline on blank paper if your instructor allows it, or do it in the answer space on screen, if you can. You can delete it after you finish answering, if space is a problem.

Some students use a "cluster" outline similar to the one illustrated below. You can also use any other pattern that works for you. This cluster outline shows the three essay skills you've reviewed so far.

Cluster Outline

Essay Skill #4: Focus Your Essay

Strive for a focused essay. The most common complaint from teachers is that essays they read are too general and don't provide adequate support for the ideas presented.

Avoid common focusing problems by following these tips:

Common Error	How to Correct It
Padding	State your main point and stick to it. Avoid all extraneous material. Follow your thesis or central point.
Weak development	Develop three main points. Provide details, examples, and/or statistics. Don't simply generalize without supporting details.
Choppiness	Use transition words to ensure that your essay is more coherent. Transition words show relationships between sentences and paragraphs. Remember that too many simple sentences give the paragraph a choppy sound.
Comma faults, fragments, run-on sentences	Put a period in place of the comma. Pay special attention to writing complete sentences and avoiding fragments. Practice sentence structure and get grammar help, if needed.

Essay Skill #5: Build Strong Paragraphs

Make sure your paragraphs have a topic sentence, which states the main idea, and a thesis, which is the central idea you're writing about. Be sure that your topic sentence relates to your thesis in an organized way. Look at this example:

Cell phones have a variety of uses: making calls, sending text messages and emails, taking photos, and other uses, depending on the phone you buy.

After you read that sentence, you expect that the writer will give more details about the various uses of cell phones. This writer's topic is the uses of cell phones, and this topic sentence states it clearly.

The sample topic sentence above could be the first sentence of an answer to questions such as the following:

► *Describe the various uses of cell phones.*

► *Compare the various uses of cell phones according to which are most useful for parents.*

► *Explain why cell phones have become so popular.*

Organizing Paragraphs

Every sentence in your paragraph should relate to the topic and thesis in some way. Remember **Skill #2: Analyze the Key Words in the Question**. Then build your paragraphs to do what the key words indicate.

There are various organizational patterns you can use for your paragraphs or essay, depending on the question. Some examples are classification, cause and effect, pros and cons, advantages and disadvantages, anecdote (short story), cataloguing, and chronological sequence.

Continue to add paragraphs as needed to answer the question completely. Your instructor may give you a limit or range for the number of paragraphs; if so, stick to that limit.

Writing a Conclusion

End with a clear conclusion. A conclusion can be two or three sentences, if you're writing a brief essay, or it can be a short paragraph of its own, if you're writing a longer essay. Your conclusion should restate the thesis and summarize your ideas. For example:

Looking at all the uses and features of cell phones I have described, it is easy to see why cell phones are so popular. They provide something for just about anyone's communication needs, are convenient to carry, and can be fun to use.

Essay Skill #6: Use Transition Words

Transition words have two purposes. They connect sentences or paragraphs. They also signal a relationship between what comes before and what goes after the transition word.

Transitions make your writing flow smoothly. Be sure to use them, but don't overdo it. Use no more than three in each paragraph, as a general rule.

Look at these examples:

Sentence structure problems can take away from the focus of an essay. Therefore, it is important to brush up on your grammar, if needed, to build your essay skills.

In conclusion, if you pay attention to the specific essay skills in this section, you can write stronger and more focused essays.

In the first example, *therefore* indicates that the first sentence is the reason for what is stated in the second sentence.

In the second example, *in conclusion* signifies that you're now writing your final paragraph or sentence.

Examples of Transition Words

therefore	furthermore	consequently
moreover	of course	on the other hand
first	in conclusion	nevertheless
since	in addition	admittedly
also	finally	thus
first of all	next	assuredly

Remember that these transition words can be used at the beginning of a sentence or in the middle, depending on what you want to emphasize; but they're less effective at the end. When the transition word come at the end of the sentence, it often fails to serve its purpose and may sound unnecessary.

For example:

▶ The human heart weighs less than a pound. On the other hand, the brain weighs three pounds [emphasis on contrast between the two organs].

▶ The human heart weighs less than a pound. The brain, on the other hand, weighs only three pounds [emphasis on the brain].

▶ The human heart weighs less than a pound. The brain weighs only three pounds, on the other hand [purpose of "on the other hand" is lost].

PRACTICE WITH TRANSITION WORDS

In this exercise, you'll review Skills #5 Build Strong Paragraphs and #6 Use Transition Words.

Write a paragraph of about five sentences using the information from the picture and text below. Incorporate at least two of the transition words from the list on the preceding page.

Your Brain...

...a three-pound universe!

You have at least 100 billion nerve cells (neurons) in your brain.

Each of these neurons makes between 5,000 and 50,000 contacts with other neurons.

Write your paragraph in this space. Include a topic sentence (main idea), transitional words and concluding sentence.

_____

_____

_____

_____

_____

_____

*Compare your answers with the author's suggested responses
in the Appendix.*

Additional Preparation Strategies

By now, you've learned specific strategies for mastering objective tests and excelling on essay exams. This part explains additional strategies you can employ to improve your preparation for taking tests in general. Let's look at these now.

Study Sheets

A study sheet has the questions on one page and the answers on another, as shown in the sample below. Or you can use one page and divide it down the middle with the questions to the left and the answers to the right.

Questions or Terms	*Terms*
1. Explain eight memory techniques (ROOSTERS)	*R*ecite aloud.
	*O*rganize the material.
	*O*ver-learn.
	*S*pread out memory work.
	*T*est and retest.
2. Why recite answers outloud?	*E*xpect to remember.
	*R*ely on the use of hooks, catchwords & so on.
	*S*tudy before sleeping.
	If you can retrieve information (recall), you have excellent control over the material. Long-term memory is improved by 80%.

Using Study Sheets

▶ After writing or reciting answers to the questions several times, you're ready to cover the answers and use a blank page to write the answers from memory.

▶ If you can answer the question correctly, without looking at the answer, place a check (√) by the question.

▶ If you can't recall the answer, look at it and try again.

▶ Repeat this process until you've mastered the material.

Study Cards

Some students use 3-by-5-inch index cards to help them study. Cards may be used for mathematics, science, English, history, or almost any academic subject. Study cards are easy to carry with you anywhere, giving you the opportunity to study whenever you have a few moments.

Some students punch a hole in the top left-hand corner of the cards and hold them all together with a metal ring. And some bookstores and office-supply stores sell "systems" for organizing cards, which include smaller cards of various colors and a notebook designed to hold the cards.

Tip: **Flash cards are especially effective for studying a foreign language or ESL (English as a Second Language).**

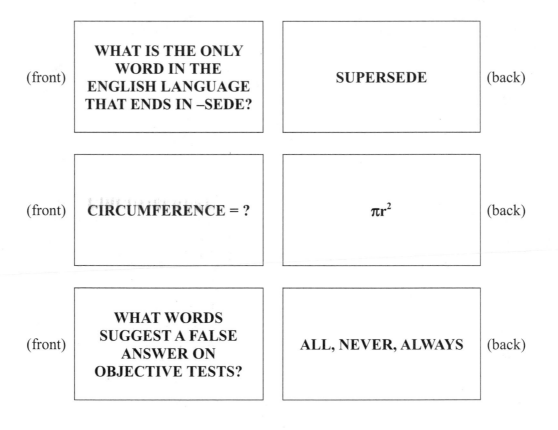

(front) **WHAT IS THE ONLY WORD IN THE ENGLISH LANGUAGE THAT ENDS IN –SEDE?** **SUPERSEDE** (back)

(front) **CIRCUMFERENCE = ?** πr^2 (back)

(front) **WHAT WORDS SUGGEST A FALSE ANSWER ON OBJECTIVE TESTS?** **ALL, NEVER, ALWAYS** (back)

Using Study Cards

1. Look at the front side of the card and ask yourself the question.

2. Answer the question or define the concept. Then turn the card over to see if you're correct.

3. Correct? Place the card in a stack to your left, or mark it somehow in pencil (so you can erase the mark later).

4. Incorrect? Test and retest three times. Put that card in a stack to your right, or mark it.

5. Have someone else ask you the questions repeating Steps 1–4.

Save Quizzes and Tests

Save every quiz or test you take. Go over the questions you missed until you're sure of the answers. Ask for assistance from your instructor, a tutor, or a study partner to help you improve before the next test. You can also use all quizzes, tests, and other papers you've written to help you review for midterms or final exams.

Remember Other Parts of Your Grade

Generally, a test score isn't the only item included in your overall grade for a class. So if you have difficulty with one test, don't give up. Use each test as a chance to review and strengthen your skills in that particular subject. At the beginning of each course, if the teacher doesn't provide information on what's required and what's counted toward the final grade, ask about it.

Exam Strategies Review

Use this list to review the exam strategies you've learned. Check [√] those you plan to practice.

For objective tests:

❑ Answer easiest questions first.

❑ Underline key words in each question.

❑ Cross out answers you've eliminated.

❑ Be alert for words such as *always* and *never*.

❑ Ensure that the grammatical structure of the answer is consistent with the question.

❑ If there's no penalty for guessing, answer every question.

For essay exams:

❑ Anticipate questions the instructor might ask.

❑ Sketch a variety of outline responses to model questions.

❑ Practice writing sample essays.

❑ Analyze the entire test, and budget your time before beginning to write.

❑ Read each question carefully, and underline key words.

❑ Create an informal cluster outline of your response before starting to write. If you choose, you can simply number your main points.

❑ Strive for a focused essay, tightly organized and supported with facts.

❑ Make sure your paragraphs have main ideas (topic sentences) and a thesis (central idea). Be sure your topic sentences relate to the thesis in your introductory paragraph in an organized way that parallels the ideas in the thesis statement.

❑ Use a paragraph structure that goes with the essay test question. Use the key words in the question as your guide.

❑ Add a conclusion to your essay or paragraph. The conclusion should relate to the essay test question.

Studying

Mathematics and

Related Subjects

Success is more a function of consistent common sense than it is of genius."

–An Wang, computer engineer, inventor, and founder of Wang Laboratories

In this part:

▶ Math Tips, Techniques, and Ideas

▶ The Five Rs of Math

▶ Tips for Computer Learning

Study Skills Strategies

Math Tips, Techniques, and Ideas

Mathematics requires special study techniques. This brief part will provide a few tips and ideas for improving your math study skills.

The ideas in this part apply to any subject in which mathematical thinking is part of the work. For example, accounting, economics, some business classes, project management, physics, engineering, and similar subjects all require mathematical thinking and learning as you study them.

Give Math Special Attention

With its abstract structures, patterns, and relationships, the study of mathematics and math-related subjects requires different techniques from those used in other subjects. Apply these guidelines to help you through the complexities:

► Copy all the instructor's theorems, principles, and definitions *exactly*. Don't paraphrase or condense anything that's written on the board. Also be sure to copy the instructor's explanation. Draw arrows to the explanation for each step of a problem.

► Because it may be difficult to take notes on the instructor's explanation and copy the problem from the board at the same time, you may want to record the instructor's explanation (always ask the instructor's permission for this). Also, ask if there are related study aids that your teacher recommends.

► Plan to spend extra time on your math homework if math is a difficult subject for you, if it's your major, or if it's a critical part of a math-related subject you're taking. Pay attention to what this might do to your study schedule and adjust as needed. Some teachers set aside part of each class to let students start homework, so students can get help with understanding concepts or difficult points. If your teacher does this, take full advantage of it.

► If math is difficult for you, you may find it necessary to ask for special help. If you become confused or lost, seek the assistance of your instructor or a tutor. Mathematics often builds on a set of rules; and if you don't understand basic principles, the likelihood is that, once you get lost, you'll stay lost. Ask for help as soon as you need it, instead of waiting until things get worse.

The Five R's of Math

Master these five techniques and you'll be well on your way to math success. You may feel that doing all these steps for every math assignment will take too much time. Indeed, it may take more time at first than you're accustomed to spending on math assignments. But stay with it—you'll soon see results in the way you learn, and you'll find it easier to study for exams.

The following pages will give you details on these five techniques and help you rate your use of them.

R1	Recopy your notes	Rewrite math notes each day in ink for clarity and permanence. Neatness is especially important because of the need for accuracy.
R2	Rework the model	This is the crucial step that most students overlook. Instead of figuring out what's being taught in the model problem, they jump right into doing homework and end up reworking problems several times. Instead, rework model problems over and over until you can do them without stopping.
R3	Recite out loud	Work with a study partner and force each other to explain out loud each step of the process.
R4	Recheck your work	Recheck your thinking process as well by listening to your "mind chatter."
R5	Reasonableness?	Does your answer to the problem make sense?

Study Groups

Jaime Escalante played a math instructor in the movie, *Stand and Deliver*. His Hispanic students all passed the Advanced Placement Mathematics exam twice in order to prove they didn't cheat on the first exam. He had students work in small groups at the board and orally explain the steps of solving a problem to each other. This was only one of his successful strategies for teaching mathematics.

THE FIVE R'S OF MATH

To help you understand the Five Rs of Math, read the descriptions in each step and write notes or recall cues under each. These notes should help you remember what's most important to you in each tip.

1. **Recopy** your notes in pen. Color-code definitions, rules, and problem areas discussed by your instructor. Neatness and legibility are your first steps toward becoming a better math student.

   How do you rate your math notes?

   ❑ Organized and clear

   ❑ Messy

   ❑ Disorganized but neat

   _____

   _____

   _____

2. **Rework** the model or example over and over until you can do it without hesitation.

   Have you ever taken this step before beginning your homework?

   ❑ Yes

   ❑ No

   If not, try it for a week and see if it makes a difference.

   _____

   _____

   _____

CONTINUED

3. **Recite.** Oral recitation will improve your mathematical skills. Practice this step with a study partner or friend. Force each other to explain out loud each step of the process. If you're studying alone, still express your thinking aloud.

Have you ever taken this step while doing your homework?

❑ Yes

❑ No

If not, try it for a week and see if it makes a difference.

_____

_____

_____

4. **Recheck** your computations. Also recheck your thinking process. This is even more important when you move from one step of a problem to the next or from one concept to a new one.

"Mind Chatter"

Questioning and recording the internal thinking of professionals revealed the following internal dialogues were common:

1. *"Let me read the question again to be sure what's being asked. I'll circle or underline the question."*

2. *"Okay. I see, but I'll read it again to be sure."*

3. *"Slow down. Don't rush."*

4. *"What's given? What's known?"*

5. *"How can I diagram, make a chart, or draw a visual to help me?"*

Lawyers, doctors, engineers, and other professionals are always painstakingly careful to reread phrases and double-check their work.

Adapted from Problem Solving and Comprehension by Arthur Whimbey and Jack Lochhead.

_____

_____

_____

5. Test for **Reasonableness.** Plug your answer into the problem to see if it makes sense. This final check could save you time and embarrassment later.

Asking questions about how reasonable an answer is will make critical thinking a habit and problem solving less ominous.

_____

_____

_____

*Compare your answers with the author's suggested responses
in the Appendix.*

TEST YOURSELF

What are the 5 "R's" of math?

_____

_____

_____

_____

_____

_____

_____

_____

Tips for Computer Learning

Computer-assisted learning works well for math and related subjects because of the specific concepts and calculations required for these subjects. Here are some suggestions for getting the most out of learning math with a computer:

▶ If your text comes with a supplementary disk, use it. It will give you extra practice and added help in learning difficult concepts.

▶ If your school has a math lab, visit it to see what's available there. Teachers or tutors may be on hand to assist you.

▶ Ask your instructor if there are any computer-assisted learning programs that could help you. Check your campus or local bookstore for added resources.

▶ If you're taking an online math course, work the problems on paper as well. This will give you added practice and help you remember what you're learning. It will also provide study notes for preparing for exams.

▶ If you need to take a math test on line, have pencils and blank paper with you, if your instructor allows. Use them to work out problems before entering your answer on the computer. On paper, you can check your answers before you submit them—something you can't always do on line, depending on the testing program.

▶ Don't count on the speed of the computer to get you through a test or assignment any faster—you still need to do all the thinking at the pace of your own brain.

Mathematics Summary

When studying for math and other related subjects, remember the Five R's of Math:

R1: **Recopy** your notes.

R2: **Rework** model problems.

R3: **Recite** aloud to explain each step of the problem-solving process.

R4: **Recheck** your work.

R5: Test your answers for **Reasonableness** –ensure that your answer makes sense.

Combine those five techniques with the following tips, and you'll be well on your way to math success.

▶ Copy all theorems, principles, and definitions carefully and exactly.

▶ Record the instructor's explanation and ask about related study aids.

▶ Plan extra time, if needed, for math homework.

▶ Ask for help as soon as you begin having problems.

▶ Use computer programs in the lab, in the library, or from a CD that comes with your textbook for extra support.

WHAT DO YOU NEED TO PRACTICE?

On the lines below, write the three most important points for you to practice from the list above.

_____

_____

_____

_____

_____

_____

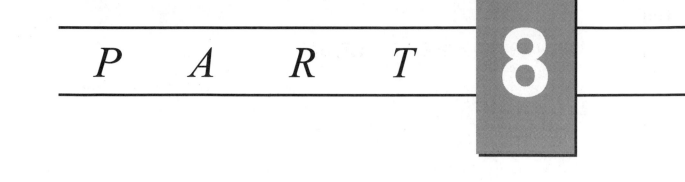

P A R T 8

Putting It All
Together

In this part:

► On Your Own

► Your Study Skill's Checklist

On Your Own

CONGRATULATIONS! You've done a lot of work on study skills and used affirmations to get to this point. To help you continue on your own, this section will take you through a review quiz, an action plan, and a checklist on study skills.

How can you continue to make progress? How can you learn to be a skillful student as well as a critical thinker? How can you use this information to improve your grades? These are all questions you want to think about as you do the review and checklist and plan your next steps for effective learning.

Notice that the following review quiz has two parts: objective questions and an essay question. As you do the quiz, remember what you learned about how to work with those two types of test questions.

FINAL REVIEW QUIZ

Choose the best possible multiple-choice, fill-in-the-blank, or true-false answer.

1. Notes should be reviewed within:

    a. 72 hours

    b. 24 hours

    c. 48 hours

    d. None of the above

2. When two opposite statements appear in a multiple-choice question:

    a. One of the opposite statements is usually correct

    b. Neither is correct

    c. Both are correct

    d. The choice in the middle is often correct

3. Recall cues are placed in the _____ margin of the paper.

4. Reciting answers to study questions improves memory by:

    a. 82%

    b. 95%

    c. 70%

    d. None of the above

5. Study time should be divided into blocks of three to four hours.

    ❑ True

    ❑ False

CONTINUED

6. All notes should be rewritten or typed except for math notes.

   ❏ True

   ❏ False

7. Visual patterns, such as trees and clocks, are useful for memorizing mathematical subjects only.

   ❏ True

   ❏ False

8. "Mind chatter" is internal dialogue used by professional problem solvers to find solutions.

   ❏ True

   ❏ False

9. Read through a paragraph before you underline or highlight.

   ❏ True

   ❏ False

10. SQ3R is a reading strategy developed for surveying and skimming easy material.

   ❏ True

   ❏ False

Compare your answers with the author's suggested responses in the Appendix.

FINAL REVIEW QUIZ: ESSAY PORTION

To do this quiz, look back through the book to find the ideas and suggestions that were most important to you for improving your study skills. Then answer the following essay questions. As you write, you'll be developing an action plan.

1. List and describe the three or four suggestions in this book that are the most important ones for you to practice.

_____

_____

_____

_____

_____

_____

_____

_____

_____

_____

2. Explain why each one is important for you, and what difference it will make in your studying.

_____

_____

_____

_____

_____

_____

_____

_____

_____

_____

_____

CONTINUED

3. Describe how and when you'll take action on this action plan. Develop an affirmation to help you.

_____

_____

_____

_____

_____

_____

_____

_____

_____

_____

You may want to show this essay to a teacher, adviser, or someone else who's helping you learn. Post a copy of your essay where you can see it, to remind you of your commitment.

Compare your answers with the author's comments in the Appendix.

Your Study Skills Checklist

This checklist is designed to help you review your study habits and get help with any areas where you need assistance. Once these problem areas have been identified, you can review sections of this book or use other resources suggested by those helping you.

You'll notice that this checklist has one set of directions for you and another set of directions for your teacher, adviser, tutor, or other helper. Follow the directions to do your work first. Then select the person who'll assist you, and ask that person to follow the directions to review your work. When both of you have finished, get together and discuss the results and any further actions that would be helpful to you.

You'll probably get more out of this checklist if you have someone else review it with you. In some circumstances, however, this may not be possible or the most practical approach. You can simply do it on your own and decide where you want to take action.

To the Student:

Go through the checklist, marking Yes or No for each question. If you need or want to take action on any item, make a check in the Action Needed column. You may want to take action on a particular item, even if you answered Yes for it; you may want to practice that skill more. On the other hand, you don't need to take action on every item you mark No; choose the items that you think are most important for you to work on.

To the Teacher, Tutor, or Adviser:

When you receive the completed checklist from your student, first review it on your own. If you differ with the student on any of the responses, note your response in a different color. If you want to emphasize any point the student has marked for action or you want to suggest action on something the student hasn't marked, then mark the Action Needed column, also with a different color.

Note: *The "I" in the questions is the student.*

CHECKLIST FOR STUDY SKILLS

Student: _____ Date: _____

Advisor/Teacher? _____ Date: _____

Tutor _____ Date: _____

Time Management	Yes	No	Action Needed
1. Do I have a weekly time schedule for classes, study, and other activities?	❏	❏	❏
2. Do I have a copy of all my course requirements, including syllabus, deadlines for papers, and dates of midterms and finals?	❏	❏	❏
3. Do I have short-term goals for my learning?	❏	❏	❏
4. Have I set aside a quiet place to study and do class work, where I have all the equipment and materials I need?	❏	❏	❏
Note Taking			
1. Do I regularly review my notes and identify strengths and weaknesses?	❏	❏	❏
2. Have I reviewed the model for recall cues, and do I use these cues for studying?	❏	❏	❏
3. Am I able to answer questions or find solutions to problems using my notes to prompt me?	❏	❏	❏
4. Have I related lecture notes to textbook or other reading assignments?	❏	❏	❏
5. Do I know and use different techniques to study my notes?	❏	❏	❏
Critical Reading Skills			
1. Do I mark my textbooks as I read them?	❏	❏	❏
2. Do I read assignments before class?	❏	❏	❏
3. Do I know the value of the SQ3R method, and if so, am I using it? If not, why not?	❏	❏	❏

SQ3R: Survey	Yes	No	Action Needed
1. Do I know how to survey the entire chapter before reading the assignment?	❏	❏	❏
SQ3R: Question			
2. Do I ask or write questions about the text as I survey?	❏	❏	❏
3. Do I then read for answers to those questions?	❏	❏	❏
4. Do I list questions I don't understand after reading the text?	❏	❏	❏
5. Do I attempt to answer all questions before going to the next topic, section, or chapter?	❏	❏	❏
SQ3R: Read and Underline			
6. Do I focus on the readings thoroughly and carefully and highlight key concepts?	❏	❏	❏
7. Can I find the topic sentences in a paragraph?	❏	❏	❏
8. Do I use highlighters for a specific purpose (e.g., vocabulary, main ideas)?	❏	❏	❏
9. Do I use special markings or symbols to identify important points or organization?	❏	❏	❏
10. Do I know how to summarize a chapter by outlining or visually organizing the material with flowcharts and the like?	❏	❏	❏
SQ3R: Recite and Write			
11. Do I understand and use recitation to help with recall and long-term memory?	❏	❏	❏
12. Do I write out questions I don't understand or can't answer?	❏	❏	❏
SQ3R: Review			
13. Do I review my reading? If so, how?	❏	❏	❏
14. Do I write study notes from my reading?	❏	❏	❏

Memory Training	Yes	No	Action Needed
1. Do I spread out my memory work instead of doing it all at once?	❏	❏	❏
2. Do I recite, over-learn, and test myself as I memorize?	❏	❏	❏
3. Do I use hooks, catchphrases, and rhymes to help me memorize?	❏	❏	❏
4. Do I create visuals to help me remember specific material?	❏	❏	❏

Exam Strategies

	Yes	No	Action Needed
1. Do I review each test question before attempting to answer it?	❏	❏	❏
2. Am I overly anxious about test taking? If so, have I found ways to help myself relax, such as slow, deep breathing?	❏	❏	❏
3. Do I budget time wisely while taking an exam?	❏	❏	❏
4. Do I answer easy questions first and go back through the exam to answer the more difficult questions last?	❏	❏	❏
5. Do I understand how to identify key words in exam directions, and do I know how to prepare a "cluster" outline for writing a 5-6 paragraph essay?	❏	❏	❏

Math and Related Subjects

	Yes	No	Action Needed
1. Do I recopy all of my notes clearly, accurately, and neatly?	❏	❏	❏
2. Do I rework the model problem over and over until I can do it easily?	❏	❏	❏
3. Do I recite explanations of problems aloud as I work—either to another or to myself?	❏	❏	❏
4. Do I recheck my computations and my thinking process?	❏	❏	❏
5. Do I test all of my work for reasonableness?	❏	❏	❏

Putting It All Together Summary

You've successfully completed the objective and essay review quizzes. Congratulations again!

If you completed the checklist with a tutor or teacher/advisor, meet with that person to discuss the results and develop an action plan to continue the progress you've made so far. If you completed the checklist alone, you can still develop an Action Plan to strengthen your study skills and reinforce your commitment to learning excellence.

Suggestion: *In a week, review the Action plan again and then, in a month, take the Check list questions again. Periodically, review parts of the book as you need them.*

Completion of this book shows that you're a determined and successful student. Remember to say, "I'm a strong, competent student."

Your Learning Strategies Coach,
Uelaine Lengefeld

A P P E N D I X

Appendix to Part 4

Comments & Suggested Responses

SQ3R Practice 1

The questions that follow are examples; there are no right or wrong answers. The important thing is that your sample questions help you focus on the key points in the text.

Two possible questions related to Step 1

1. Why is surveying important?

2. How do I survey a chapter?

Two possible questions related to Step 2

1. How do I create questions from the heading of a section?

2. What words can I use to help me make up questions?

SQ3R Practice 2

1. Two possible questions related to the text:

   Question one: What can you use to help guide you when you recite?

   Question two: What's the best way to recite?

Your suggested questions may be somewhat different from these, but see if yours contain the important ideas in the text: a description of Step 4, the information that can help you with this step, how to recite, and the value of recall cues.

Use these same ideas to guide you as you check your work for the rest of the exercise.

2. Suggested markings and recall cues for the text:

Step 4, Recite **Use markings** **Always do it!**	Once you have formed questions on your reading and have read to answer those questions, you're ready to <u>recite the answers</u>. <u>Use your underlining and markings</u> to guide you. Reciting <u>helps you learn and remember</u> what you've read. Don't skip this step, even if you think you know the information. This step will make a big difference in how well you master the material.
Recite, make notes	Recite the answers out loud (or quietly to yourself). Also write <u>brief study notes</u>, which will <u>help encode</u> the information in your long-term memory for easier retrieval on the final examination.
Hard? Write summary	Write a sentence summary of the main idea in each paragraph if the material is extremely difficult for you.
Recall cues save time	<u>The recall cues you wrote in the margins are an essential step</u>. If you use those cues to recite, you may not need study notes for some classes.

3. The following are suggested answers to the questions formulated in the first segment of this exercise. Your answers should go with whatever questions you wrote for that segment.

   Question one: What can you use to help guide you when you recite?

   Suggested answer: You can use your markings and recall cues as guides for reciting.

   Question two: What's the best way to recite?

   Suggested answer: Recite out loud, if possible (or quietly to yourself).

Appendix to Part 5

Comments & Suggested Responses

Find a Pattern

The numbers in the sequence are the first 7 multiples of 3: 3 (3 x 1), 6 (3 x 2), 9 (3 x 3), 12 (3 x 4), 15 (3 x 5), 18 (3 x 6), and 21 (3 x 7).

Appendix to Part 6

Comments & Suggested Responses

Essay Exam Matching Quiz

1. F	8. D
2. N	9. M
3. K	10. A
4. H	11. L
5. G	12. E
6. I	13. B
7. J	14. C

If you're still unsure about the meanings of some of these words, look them up in a dictionary. They're important words in most essay tests and assignments.

Practice with Transition Words

An amazing amount of activity goes on in the human brain. There are at least 100 billion nerve cells, or neurons, in your brain. Moreover, each of these neurons is busy making between 5,000 and 50,000 contacts with other neurons! Thus you can consider the brain a small universe, for it does all this and yet weighs only three pounds.

Your paragraph may look different. The important thing is that you used the main ideas: the size of the brain compared with the number of neurons and the amount of activity it contains. You also needed to use two transition words somewhere in the paragraph to help connect the ideas.

The transition words used in the sample above are *moreover* and *thus*. Which transition words did you use?

Appendix to Part 7

Comments & Suggested Responses

The Five R's of Math

1. Recall cues for R1:

    Neat clear copy

    Can use color

2. Recall cues for R2:

    Do the model

    Over and over!

3. Recall cues for R3:

    Recite

    Explain every step

4. Recall cues for R4:

    Recheck

    Think

    Think again!

5. Recall cues for R5:

    Does it make sense?

You may have used some different recall cues. The important point is to help you remember these five important steps for learning math and related subjects.

Appendix to Part 8

Comments & Suggested Responses

Final Review Quiz

1. **B**   Review class notes as soon as possible, certainly within 24 hours, so that you can clarify abbreviations and garbled notes.

2. **A**   Often one of two opposite statements is correct in a multiple-choice question.

3. **Left**   Recall cues are placed in the left-hand margin.

4. **D**   "None of the above" is correct; the actual answer is 80%.

5. **F**   Study time is best broken into intervals of an hour to an hour and a half, with 10-minute breaks.

6. **F**   Instead of recopying notes, spend your study time writing study questions and recall phrases and reciting answers out loud. Math notes, however, should be recopied.

7. **F**   Visual organizers, such as trees and maps, can be used in any subject.

8. **T**   Professional problem solvers think methodically and talk themselves through the problem.

9. **T**   To avoid too much underlining, read a paragraph first and then underline the important points when you reread it.

10. **F**   SQ3R is for reading difficult or complex material.

Did you get 100% correct? If not, go back into the text to get more information and review the material for those you missed, especially if you scored 70% or less (7 answers or fewer correct).

Final Review Quiz: Essay Portion

Because your essay is about your individual needs and goals, a sample isn't included here. But do check the quality of your essay and your action plan using the following questions:

1. Did you start your essay with an introduction that describes the main point of the essay (thesis).

2. Does each paragraph have a topic sentence?

3. Did each paragraph give some detail about the suggestion?

4. Did you talk about why the suggestion is important to you?

5. Did you describe how the suggestion will help with your studying?

6. Did you finish with specific details in the conclusion about when and how you'll put these suggestions into practice?

Additional Reading

Crisp 50-Minute Series books:

Andrus, Carol. *Fat-Free Writing*.

Bonet, Diana. *The Business of Listening*.

Feldman, Daniel A. *Critical Thinking*.

Haynes, Marion E. *Time Management*.

Riley, Lorna. *Achieving Results*.

Steinbach, Robert. *Successful Lifelong Learning*.

KAZ® (Keyboarding A-Z).

Other related reading:

Banner, James M., and Harold C. Cannon. *The Elements of Learning*. New Haven, CT: Yale University Press, 1999.

Fry, Ron. *How to Study*. Boston, MA: Thomson Learning/Delmar, 2005.

———. *Improve Your Reading*. Boston, MA: Thomson Learning/Delmar, 2005.

Funk, Wilfred, and Norman Lewis. *Thirty Days to a More Powerful Vocabulary*. NY: Pocket Books, 2003.

Luckie, William R., Wood Smethurst, and Sara Beth Huntley. *Study Power Workbook*. Brookline, MA: Brookline Books, 2000.

Whimbey, Arthur, and Jack Lochhead. *Problem Solving and Comprehension, Sixth Edition*. Mahwah, NJ: Lawrence Erlbaum Associates, 1999